T H E

10

Things You
Should Know
About the

CREATION VS.
EVOLUTION
DEBATE

RON RHODES

HARVEST HOUSE PUBLISHERS

EUGENE, OREGON

Cover by Terry Dugan Design, Minneapolis, Minnesota

THE 10 THINGS YOU SHOULD KNOW ABOUT THE CREATION VS.
EVOLUTION DEBATE
Copyright © 2004 by Ron Rhodes
Published by Harvest House Publishers
Eugene, Oregon 97402
www.harvesthousepublishers.com

Library of Congress Cataloging-in-Publication Data

Rhodes, Ron.
    The 10 things you should know about the creation vs. evolution debate / Ron Rhodes.
      p. cm.
    Includes bibliographical references.
    ISBN 0-7369-1152-9 (pbk.)
    1. Creationism. 2. Evolution—Religious aspects—Christianity. 3. Evolution (Biology)—Religious
aspects—Christianity. I. Title: Ten things you should know about the creation vs. evolution debate.
II. Title.
BS651.R523 2004
231.7'652—dc22   2003018829

Printed in the United States of America

04 05 06 07 08 09 10 11 / BP-MS / 10 9 8 7 6 5 4 3 2 1

To David, with affection

Acknowledgments

I researched and wrote this book during a time when I was extraordinarily busy with various ministry activities. Only through the sacrificial and prayerful support of my family—Kerri, David, and Kylie—was I able to finish the project in a reasonable time frame. I want to pay a special thanks to David, who assisted in typing. His efforts are appreciated.

Contents

The Creation vs. Evolution Debate:

Why It Matters

Ape-men, dinosaurs, evolution, and the big bang theory (which postulates that our universe began billions of years ago with a single explosion) are fascinating to the modern mind. Even in the relatively short time I took to write this book, I came across one article after another in various newspapers and magazines that addressed one or more of these issues. Small discoveries seem to be reported in the media as big news.

For example, I came across an article entitled "New Evidence Gives Credence to the Big-Bang Theory" in which the author claimed, "Details now show that the universe is 13.7 billion years old, with an uncertainty of only 1 percent."[1] The article goes on to tell us about all the strange materials our universe is composed of.

Another article reported the discovery of alleged 350,000-year-old footprints of what paleontologists call "Stone Age man." We are told that the footprints "were made by three early, upright-walking humans as they descended the treacherous side of a volcano—perhaps to escape an eruption." This discovery was said to add "another cog in the connect between ourselves and our ancestors."[2]

Yet another fascinating article I came across claims that some dinosaurs were cannibals. "When food and water were scarce, scientists believe majungatholus fed on the remains of other dinosaurs like titanosaurs—gigantic, long-necked plant-eaters—and even scavenged the carcasses of its own dead." Furthermore, "New fossil evidence suggests a distant cousin of the tyrannosaurus that roamed the plains of Madagascar millions of years ago regularly dined on its own kind to survive during hard times."[3]

Yet another article entitled "T-Rex, Merciless Killer or Garbage Disposal Unit?" suggests that the towering Tyrannosaurus Rex may have been a scavenger that lived on rotting corpses, or perhaps just ate the prey of smaller dinosaurs. "I believe it was a scavenger pure and simple because I can't find any evidence to support the theory that it was a predator," paleontologist Jack Horner said. Horner was the inspiration for scientist Alan Grant—played by Sam Neill—in Steven Spielberg's *Jurassic Park*. Horner suggested that the lumbering giant was "too slow, its arms too small, and its sight too poor to catch anything moving."[4]

Despite the obvious interest people have in evolution and all things ancient, a very small percentage of Americans actually *believe* in evolution and its related doctrines. Current estimates are that only about 10 percent of the people in the United States believe that Charles Darwin's theory of evolution is true. This small group believes God played absolutely no role in man's emergence on planet earth. The rest of the American public believe either in biblical creationism or in what has come to be called theistic evolution, which argues that evolution was a process guided by God (I address this theory later in the book).[5]

Why so few believers in evolution? Phillip E. Johnson, in his book *Defeating Darwinism by Opening Minds*, suggests that "the people suspect that what is being presented to them as 'scientific fact' consists largely of an ideology that goes far beyond the scientific evidence."[6] The ideology Johnson speaks of is primarily naturalism—the idea that all phenomena in the universe can be explained wholly in terms of natural causes and laws. Because naturalism is the undergirding philosophy of evolutionary theory, I have devoted an entire chapter of this book to examining it in detail (see chapter 2).

Charles Darwin and *On the Origin of Species*

When and where did the creation-evolution debate emerge? Actually, various forms of evolutionism have been around for a very long time, far before Charles Darwin was even born. Indeed, some of the early Greeks believed in a form of evolution. Anaximander (610–545 B.C.) was convinced that human beings had evolved from fish. Empedocles (490–430 B.C.), another Greek, believed animals evolved from plants.[7] Aristotle, a Greek philosopher and tutor of Alexander the Great, believed in an evolutionary process from simple to complex life-forms brought about by a "tendency within," though he also believed in a "mover" or "designer."[8] Since then, many individuals throughout history have held to some form of evolutionary theory (space forbids a detailed account of these).

In the late eighteenth and early nineteenth centuries, one individual who did significant research on evolution, and who for a brief time overlapped with Charles Darwin, was Chevalier de Lamarck (1744–1829), author of *Zoological Philosophy*. Lamarck believed that a creature could develop new organs as a result of a new need the creature developed. He believed that all life-forms had within them an inner innate drive toward increased complexity, improvement, and progress.[9] An example of this, Lamarck said, was giraffes who lived in a drought-plagued terrain and, over generations, grew longer necks so they could reach leaves high up on the trees. He also believed that any such change that occurred in a creature during its lifetime would be

transmitted to its offspring through the natural process of reproduction.[10]

The most celebrated of all evolutionists was Charles Darwin,
who wrote the greatly controversial *On the Origin of Species*—
a book that brought the creation-evolution debate to a fever pitch.
Indeed, within just ten years of its publication, Darwinism
became widely accepted in England and shortly thereafter blos-
somed in continental Europe and the United States.

Darwin, so well-known for evolutionism, acknowledges in
his autobiography that he was once a creationist, though this
shouldn't be taken to mean he was a devout Christian who
believed in biblical inerrancy.[11] Even prior to writing *On the
Origin of Species,* Darwin had "honest and conscientious doubts"
about Christianity, which he expressed to his wife, Emma.[12] He
says he *wanted* to believe in the afterlife but found the evidence
for Christianity unconvincing. Emma was greatly disturbed by
all this. Darwin's faith in Christianity waned as his evolutionist views gained strength.[13]

Heavily influenced by David Hume (who wrote an
academic treatise against miracles and the supernatural),[14] Darwin
increasingly came to distrust the Bible and found more and more
problems with anything supernatural. In his autobiography,
Darwin argued "that the clearest evidence would be requisite to
make any sane man believe in miracles by which Christianity
is supported—that the more we know of the fixed laws of nature
the more incredible do miracles become—that the men of that
time [in biblical history] were ignorant and credulous to a degree
almost incomprehensible by us—that the Gospels cannot be
proved to have been written simultaneously with the events—
that they differ in many important details, far too important as
it seemed to me to be admitted as the usual inaccuracies of eyewit-
nesses."[15] Darwin's confidence in Christianity plummeted.[16]

The problem of evil ("why do bad things happen to good
people") caused Darwin's confidence in Christianity to further

erode, especially when his beloved ten-year-old daughter, Annie, died in 1851. In *Annie's Box: Charles Darwin, His Daughter, and Human Evolution,* written by Randal Keynes (the great-great-grandson of Charles Darwin), we read that "when Annie fell ill, Darwin was at her bedside day and night, doing all he could for her, making copious notes about her deteriorating health, bringing her 'beautifully good' tea." The pain of losing his daughter "cast a shadow over Darwin's thinking about the natural world and the struggle for life. Her death also inflamed the mental turmoil over religion and the existence of God that he had experienced since his return from the voyage of HMS *Beagle* [a voyage during which he did evolutionary research]."[17] Keynes notes that "after Annie's death, Charles set the Christian faith firmly behind him. He did not attend church services with the family; he walked with them to the church door, but left them to enter on their own."[18] Darwin solidified his views on naturalistic evolution during this time.

Eight years later, in 1859, Darwin wrote *On the Origin of Species,* which has been called "one of the most important books ever written" and "a book that shook the world."[19] In this book, Darwin spoke of the differences between members of a particular species. This is called "variation." Darwin taught that more members are born in each species than can possibly survive to adult maturity. In view of limited resources, each member of a species must compete with other members of the same species for survival. Those who survive and mature to adulthood are simply the fittest in that species. This is called the "survival of the fittest."

Darwin subsequently argued that these fit members of the species passed on their fitness to their descendants by positive mutations. As this process continued over millions (possibly billions) of years, guided by "natural selection," not only changes in individual species but also entirely new species emerged. This is the heart of evolutionary theory.

Origins and Worldviews

Certainly an important reason why the creation-evolution debate matters is that a person's view of his own origins will profoundly affect not only the way he looks at himself but also his general attitude toward other people. It will affect his personal sense of morality,[20] as well as his worldview and personal philosophy of life.[21] In short, whether a person thinks he was specially created by God or was just a cosmic accident will play a large role in molding who he is for the rest of his life.

Without a God who created us, we are just the chance product (or cosmic accident) of random mutations over billions of years, and humanity is not unique. We are not responsible to God and have no divine commandments to obey.[22] All this talk about sin and repentance is just a lot of hot air. We have no need for a Savior, no need to trust in Christ. Man is the master of his own destiny; he is his own god. Ultimately, life has no real purpose. Man is adrift in a purposeless universe.[23] This life is all that exists, and we have no afterlife to look forward to. We will face no future judgment. In short, as Cornell biologist William Provine put it, Darwinism implies "no life after death, no ultimate foundation for ethics, no ultimate meaning for life."[24]

On the other hand, if a Creator does exist, we are *not* accidents, and we are *meant* to be here. If creationism is the correct view, man *does* have a purpose in life, and that purpose is to serve the Creator. We are responsible to govern our lives according to the revelation given to us by the Creator (the Bible). Man will one day have to give an accounting to the Creator for his actions. Man is *not* the master of his own fate. Man is a creature responsible to the Creator. And in view of man's sin problem, man is very much in need of a Savior. Quite obviously, then, the creation-evolution debate matters a great deal.

For Christians, I can point to further reasons why the debate matters. For example, if evolution is correct, then the book of

Genesis must be mere myth. And if the book of Genesis cannot be trusted, how can the rest of the Bible be trusted? Genesis is foundational to the rest of the Bible, and if it is fictional, then the rest of Scripture is undermined as well.

Certainly portions of the New Testament would seem impossible to believe if the book of Genesis proved to be fictional. After all, quite a number of verses in the New Testament directly refer to the creation account and give every indication of accepting its historicity (for example, see Luke 3:38; Romans 5:14; 1 Corinthians 11:9; 15:22; 2 Corinthians 11:3; 1 Timothy 2:13-14). All in all, more than 60 verses in the New Testament either quote from or allude to the first three chapters of Genesis.[25] If Genesis is myth, what do we make of these verses?

Further, what do we make of Jesus Christ, who Himself accepted the account of the creation of Adam and Eve (Matthew 19:4; Mark 10:6; see also Genesis 1:27; 2:24) as well as the historicity of the flood during Noah's time (Matthew 24:38; Luke 17:27)? If Jesus was wrong about this, then how can we trust anything else He said in the New Testament? As one Christian scholar put it, "If Genesis is not historically dependable, then Jesus is not a dependable guide to all truth, and we are without a savior."[26]

Conversely, however, if Jesus *is* God and is therefore omniscient (all-knowing), then His confirmation of the creation account in Genesis serves as a powerful stamp of approval that Genesis is not myth but is historically dependable. More than one Christian scholar has observed that Jesus often seems to have specifically given credence to portions of the Old Testament that would one day be undermined and scorned by critics (see, for example, Matthew 19:4 and Luke 17:29).[27]

The Atheistic Underpinnings of Evolutionary Theory

Earlier in the chapter I documented how evolutionism caused Darwin to lose his faith. Since his day, Darwin's experience has been repeated numerous times in the lives of many people. Philosopher Huston Smith has suggested that evolutionary theory has caused more people to lose religious faith than any other factor.[28] Philosopher Daniel Dennett has approvingly spoken of Darwinism as a "universal acid" that corrodes traditional spirituality.[29] "Like universal acid, the theory of evolution eats through just about every traditional religious idea."[30]

Of course, all this is good news for atheists, who hold to the philosophy of naturalism. In fact, one atheist boasts that Darwinism enables a person to be an "intellectually fulfilled atheist."[31] Such atheists find no need for supernatural explanations regarding man's origin. As stated in the *Humanist Manifesto II* (signed by such luminaries as author Isaac Asimov, psychologist B.F. Skinner, and ethicist Joseph Fletcher), "We find insufficient evidence for belief in the existence of a supernatural; it is either meaningless or irrelevant to the question of the survival and fulfillment of the human race. As nontheists, we begin with humans not God, nature not deity."[32]

Such atheists have no need for God to bring meaning to man's origins and man's current life. In his book, *What Is Secular Humanism?* Dr. James Hitchcock states:

> Groups like the American Humanist Association are not humanists just in the sense that they have an interest in the humanities or that they value man over nature.… In their self-definition, God does not exist.… They promote a way of life that systematically excludes God and all religion in the traditional sense. Man, for better or worse, is on his own in the universe. He marks the highest point to which nature has yet evolved, and he must rely entirely on his own resources.[33]

Isaac Asimov, one of the most prolific authors and science writers of all time, is bluntly honest regarding his disbelief in God:

I am an atheist, out and out. It took me a long time to say it. I've been an atheist for years and years, but somehow I felt it was intellectually unrespectable to say one was an atheist, because it assumed knowledge that one didn't have. Somehow it was better to say one was a humanist or an agnostic. I finally decided that I'm a creature of emotion as well as of reason. Emotionally I am an atheist. I don't have the evidence to prove that God doesn't exist, but I so strongly suspect he doesn't that I don't want to waste my time.[34]

Likewise, famous evolutionary scientist Carl Sagan asserted at the beginning of his *Cosmos* television series on PBS, "The Cosmos is all that is or ever was or ever will be."[35] In other words, we need not concern ourselves with any deity.

Evolutionists scoff at the idea that a Creator brought things into being. Asimov tells us that the "universe can be explained by evidence obtained from the Universe alone...no supernatural agency need be called upon."[36] The explanation of man's origin is always the theory of evolution.

Frederick Edwords, in an article published in *The Humanist* magazine, explains man's origin this way:

Human beings are neither entirely unique from other forms of life nor are they the final product of some planned scheme of development.... All life forms are constructed from the same basic elements, the same sorts of atoms, as are nonliving substances.... Humans are the current result of a long series of natural evolutionary changes, but not the only result or the final one. Continuous change can be expected to affect ourselves, other life forms, and the cosmos as a whole. There appears to be no ultimate beginning or end to this process.[37]

Humanists have even produced children's books that argue against any role for a Creator-God. Most children today are aware of the Berenstain Bears books. In one of these books, Papa Bear explains to his son that "Nature is you, nature is me. It's all that is or was or ever will be."[38] These words sound amazingly similar to Sagan's: "The Cosmos is all that is or ever was or ever will be."[39]

Humanist Chris Brockman wrote a children's book entitled, *What About Gods?* In this book we read, "We no longer need gods to explain how things happen. By careful thinking, measuring, and testing we have discovered many of the real causes of things, and we're discovering more all the time. We call this thinking."[40]

Of course, such humanists see no divine purpose for humanity in the world. The *Humanist Manifesto II* asserts, "We can discover no divine purpose or providence for the human species. While there is much that we do not know, humans are responsible for what we are or will become. No deity will save us; we must save ourselves."[41] In other words, we are all alone in this great big universe, with no ultimate purpose or destiny.

Nor is there an afterlife to look forward to. In his book *Forbidden Fruit: The Ethics of Humanism,* humanist leader Paul Kurtz said that "the theist's world is only a dream world; it is a feeble escape into a future that will never come."[42] Kurtz also stated, "Promises of immortal salvation or fear of eternal damnation are both illusory and harmful. They distract humans from present concerns, from self-actualization, and from rectifying social injustices." He asserts: "There is no credible evidence that life survives the death of the body. We continue to exist in our progeny and in the way that our lives have influenced others in our culture."[43] In other words, as we continue to evolve, we will hopefully pass on to our descendants positive virtues and characteristics. *And that's the end of it!*

What a tragic worldview! I think I am safe in saying, however, that some of recent history's most well-known atheistic evolutionists—men like Isaac Asimov, Carl Sagan, and Stephen Jay Gould—have had a sobering change of heart on all this, since they are no longer among the land of the living. What a horrible thing it must be to believe in and dogmatically teach atheistic evolution—denying the Creator-God's existence—only to die and suddenly realize that your entire life was spent defending a lie.

Darwinism and Social Injustice

Another reason why the creation-evolution debate matters is that evolutionary theory has had a detrimental effect on society, including (but not limited to) providing a philosophical foundation and justification for such social injustices as Nazism, racism, and sexism.

Nazism. Many people may be unaware of the connection between Adolf Hitler and evolutionism. Hitler was a Darwinian evolutionist, and he sought to implement a "survival of the fittest" philosophy in Germany.[44] How ironic that in the struggle for the survival of the fittest, Hitler and his Nazi thugs were apparently proven the weaker.[45]

Evolutionists are quick to point out that Darwin's theory of natural selection cannot be criticized simply because it has been perverted by some.[46] While this point may have some merit, the fact remains that evolution and the naturalism that undergirds it serve as a philosophical platform that enables such abuses to easily emerge.

Racism. Evolutionary theory has certainly played a role in fostering racism. At one time in United States history, Congress passed a bill that authorized the U.S. Census Bureau to count each slave as three-fifths of a person. This Congressional compromise resulted in what one African American writer of the 1890s

called "the 'Inferior Race Theory,' the placing of the Negro some-
where between the barnyard animals and human beings."[47] This
racist outrage took place just two decades after Darwin published
On the Origin of Species.

Some whites in those days tried to argue that blacks were
less than human. Buckner H. Payne, in his book *The Negro:
What Is His Ethnological Status?* (published in the decade following *The Origin of Species*), argued that "since blacks are present with us today, they must have been in the ark. There were
only eight souls saved in the ark, however, and they are fully
accounted for by Noah's family. As one of the beasts in the ark,
the black has no soul to be saved."[48]

This same racist attitude has been manifest by a number of
well-known evolutionists, such as Thomas Huxley. Even Charles
Darwin believed a time was coming in the not-too-distant future
when the lower races of man would be eliminated by the higher
civilized races.[49]

Sexism. Darwin must not have been too popular among the
women of his day, for his evolutionary views certainly contained
a sexist element. Darwin argued that men had substantially
greater mental powers than do women, and therefore men are
more prone to attain a higher eminence in whatever undertaking
they attempt.[50] Of course, Darwin's statement has proved to be
incorrect in the real world in which women have attained
eminence equal to that of their male counterparts.

The Need for Intelligent Faith

Yet another reason the creation-evolution debate is important is that it has called attention to the fact that both Christianity
and evolution are faith systems. Too often the creation-evolution
debate has been portrayed as a *faith*-based system (creation) in
opposition to a *fact*-based system (evolution). But *both* systems
are, in reality, faith-based.

Duane T. Gish, a well-known creationist, has pointed out that the introduction to Charles Darwin's *On the Origin of Species*, written by a British biologist and evolutionist, includes a statement that "belief in the theory of evolution is thus exactly parallel to belief in special creation—both are concepts which believers know to be true but neither, up to the present, has been capable of proof."[51] If a system is incapable of proof, then its believers must exercise faith.

The fact is that no living scientists have empirically observed simple life-forms evolving into complex life-forms over billions of years of time. If positive mutations and natural selection have never been empirically observed, then the basic evidence for evolution rests on faith and not observed fact.[52] This means that evolutionism is every bit as much a faith system as is creationism. The pivotal question becomes, Which faith system has the better evidence to back it up? That is the question I seek to answer throughout this book.

Stereotypes and False Caricatures

Before I address arguments in favor of creationism in subsequent chapters in this book, I must briefly touch on the stereotypes and caricatures of creationists that evolutionists often set forth. My goal is simply to let you know what to expect if you choose to engage an evolutionist in debate.

1. *Creationism is religious in nature and is therefore to be excluded from serious consideration.* This stereotype effectively marginalizes creationism without even refuting it. Marginalizing an idea has become effective in our times because of the prevalence of the mind-set that religion does not belong in schools and other public institutions.[53]

Evolutionists, of course, are not being consistent. For instance, a few of the Ten Commandments—those prohibiting murder, false witness, and stealing—are identical to laws in the law code of our country. The fact that these commandments are in the Bible (and are therefore "religious" in nature) is no reason to marginalize them and exclude them from serious attention in public institutions. In keeping with this, no public school would eliminate behavioral rules such as "no stealing" and "no cheating" simply because of similar commandments in the Bible.[54] More than one Christian apologist has noted the inconsistency in excluding creationism from serious consideration because it is "religious" when in fact evolutionism favors the religious position of secular humanism. If creationism is excluded for religious considerations, evolutionism should likewise be excluded.

2. *Creationism is a view held only by religious extremists and is therefore to be excluded from serious consideration.* Most people in this country have seen the movie *Inherit the Wind*. In this movie, evolutionists are portrayed as enlightened intellects while creationists are portrayed as religious extremists. One walks away from the movie with the feeling that creationists are pitifully and sadly misled individuals and that creationism is something no respectable person with an ounce of brains should have anything to do with. The movie ignores the fact that some of the greatest scientists the world has ever known have been creationists, including the likes of Robert Boyle, Isaac Newton, and Louis Pasteur.

By portraying creationists as religious nuts, evolutionists have been extremely successful in spinning their viewpoint in a favorable light, especially in the media. Evolutionists use the same technique that some politicians use when their embarrassing failures become public. Politicians are experts at drawing attention away from their embarrassments and presenting themselves in a favorable light. Evolutionists likewise seek to draw attention away from their embarrassment—that is, their lack of evidence for evolutionary theory (no intermediate fossils, no evidence for an ongoing series of positive mutations, no effective argument against intelligent design)—by making creationists look like extremists.[55]

3. *Creationism is unscientific and is therefore to be excluded from serious consideration.* Evolutionists Dylan Evans and Howard Selina argue that "there is nothing scientific about 'creation science.' It is not supported by the evidence or by good argument."[56] Creationist (and scientist) Hugh Ross has pointed out that the National Center for Science Education has long taught that science is "empirically based and necessarily materialist," that "miracles cannot be allowed," and that "any theory with a supernatural foundation is not scientific."[57] Since creationism obviously involves the miracle of God creating the universe by the power of His Word, creationism is stamped "unscientific" and excluded from serious consideration. (I present evidence for the possibility of miracles in chapter 2 of this book.)

4. *Creationism is an enemy of education and is therefore to be excluded from serious consideration.* Because creationists want creationism taught in public schools as an alternative to evolution, creationists are caricatured as enemies of education because they want *myth* to be taught alongside *fact*. Creationists are therefore portrayed as enemies of education.[58] (The folly of this ridiculous claim will become clear in subsequent chapters.)

5. *Creationism involves fairy tales believed by stupid people and is therefore to be excluded from serious consideration.* Well-known evolutionist Richard Dawkins is not shy about making his feelings known: "It is absolutely safe to say that if you meet somebody who claims not to believe in evolution, that person is ignorant, stupid or insane (or wicked, but I'd rather not consider that)."[59] This brazen ad hominem argument shows the disdain that many evolutionists have for creationists and ignores many intelligent arguments for creationism.

Such caricatures are unfortunate, but they are a very real part of the creation-evolution debate. I suggest that the best policy is to focus objective attention on the primary issues of the debate—issues such as the fossil evidence, evidence that mutations are generally harmful, evidence related to the second law of thermodynamics, evidence for intelligent design, and the like. This approach effectively keeps the debate out of the arena of subjective emotionalism and seeks to generate more light than heat.

Of course, people will ultimately believe what they want to believe. Nevertheless, because debates involve the exchange of arguments, and because arguments can alter an open-minded person's worldview, the creation-evolution debate is a worthy one. In each chapter of this book, I will seek to deal with one primary issue in the debate.

1

There Are Different Kinds of Evolution

As a teenage boy, I remember being taught in school that evolution was a proven scientific fact. I was taught the doctrine of the "survival of the fittest"—the idea that the fittest members of each individual species would survive and mature to adulthood, and that these "fit members" would, by positive genetic mutations, pass on this "fitness" to their descendants. I was taught that this process had been going on for billions of years and through this process, not only did individual species improve, but entirely *new* species emerged as well. I was taught that the theory of evolution proved that human beings and modern apes evolved from a common ancestor, the clear implication being that the Genesis account of creation was nothing but mere myth.

As I continued my education throughout high school, evolution was never presented as an optional belief but was always assumed to be true. At age 17, however, I became a Christian—and started to challenge some of the basic assumptions I had uncritically accepted. Among these assumptions were the various proofs for evolution and the naturalistic philosophy that undergirded it.

One thing that became very clear to me early on was that a great deal of confusion exists regarding what the term *evolution* means. A common dictionary definition of the word is "a process of developing" or "gradual development." In this broad sense, creationists can agree with evolution. For example, I might speak about the evolution (the gradual development) of the book I am writing. Certainly it took some time to develop. Or I might read about the evolution (the gradual development) of the airplane by the Wright brothers. Nothing is wrong or offensive about this use of the word *evolution.*

Of course, Darwinian evolutionists use the term much more specifically. They view evolution as the theory that "millions of years ago lifeless matter, acted upon by natural forces, gave origin to one or more minute living organisms which have since evolved into all living and extinct plants and animals including man."[1] In other words, evolution is a naturalistic theory that proposes that simple life-forms evolved into complex life-forms by chance and random variation, with species giving rise to new species over billions of years. Ultimately, this means that all living things—including human beings and apes—are related to each other in that they have a common ancestor.[2] As evolutionists Dylan Evans and Howard Selina put it, "Ultimately, every species on Earth is descended from a single common ancestor, just as the branches on a tree all spring from a single trunk."[3]

In evolutionary theory, natural selection, mutations, and long periods of time play a significant role. Natural selection may be defined as "preferential survival of individuals having advantageous variations relative to other members of their population or species."[4] That may sound complicated, but evolutionist Michael Benton suggests four basic propositions that bring clarity to the issue:

1. Organisms produce more offspring than can survive and reproduce.

2. The organisms that survive tend to be better adapted to local environments.

3. The characters of the parent appear in the offspring.

4. So generation by generation, hundreds of thousands of times over, the better-adapted lines will survive to pass on the features that give them advantage in local environments.[5]

What all this means is that nature produces far more offspring in any given species than can possibly survive. Because of limited resources, these offspring must compete with each other to survive. This competition has winners and losers. The winners are those who are best fit to survive in that environment, and the losers are the least fit. As time passes, the winners pass on their superior traits (*survival* traits) to their offspring so they too can survive. As this process continues over many generations—with losers continually weeded out and the superior traits of the winners passed down to offspring through positive mutations—evolution occurs.[6] "Over the course of many generations the advantageous gene (and its corresponding trait) will be found in a higher proportion of individuals."[7]

In view of this, some evolutionists actually define natural selection as "the process by which in every generation individuals of lower fitness are removed from the population."[8] Simply put, natural selection involves a "process of elimination."[9]

An example sometimes cited to illustrate natural selection is the insulating coat of the polar bear. We are told that at some point during the polar bear's evolution, a thick insulating coat developed in response to the cold environment, and this "advantage" was passed on to future offspring by positive mutations, while polar bears less adapted to the environment were weeded out (they did not survive).[10]

This understanding of evolution is based entirely on naturalism, the idea that all phenomena in the world can be explained in terms of natural causes and laws. Naturalism effectively takes God out of the picture. As one evolutionist put it, "once we accept the theory of evolution by natural selection, the traditional idea of God really does go out of the window."[11] A modern science textbook pointedly states that "living creatures on earth are a direct product of the earth. There is every reason to believe that living things owe their origin entirely to certain physical and chemical properties of the ancient earth." The textbook goes on to assert that "nothing supernatural appeared to be involved—only time and natural physical and chemical laws operating within the peculiarly suitable environment."[12] This naturalistic outlook is the foundational philosophy of evolution. (I address naturalism in detail in the next chapter and natural selection in chapter 6.)

The Assumptions of Evolution

Evolutionary theory accepts at least five basic assumptions. As you consider these assumptions, I suggest that you pay special attention to their speculative nature (that is, the assumptions have no genuine scientific proof behind them):

1. *Nonliving things gave rise to living things.* Somehow, in some way, "spontaneous generation" occurred at some point in the unimaginably distant past, and all of a sudden, life emerged. After this initial life emerged from nonlife, some 1.7 million highly complex species eventually evolved.[13]

2. *Simple life-forms evolved into increasingly complex life-forms.* For example, the protozoa (single-celled, microscopic organisms) gave rise to the metazoa (multicellular animals with organs), the invertebrates (lacking a backbone) gave rise to the vertebrates (having a backbone), within the vertebrates the fish

gave rise to amphibia, the amphibia gave rise to reptiles, reptiles gave rise to birds and mammals, and so on.

3. *All of this was the product of chance.* No deity was involved. No supernatural providence was involved. Human beings and all life-forms on planet earth are essentially a cosmic accident that took place purely by natural causes.

4. *All this took place over aeons and aeons of time.* Billions of years were necessary for simple life-forms to evolve into complex life-forms. Evolutionists argue that "the effect of numerous instances of selection leads to a species being modified over time."[14] Indeed, "Given enough time, there could be a series of many small steps linking a monkey ancestor to a human descendant."[15]

Most evolutionists believe that our solar system emerged around five billion years ago, and that simple life-forms emerged on planet earth from nonliving chemicals perhaps four billion years ago. Since this time, increasingly complex life-forms have evolved. Man finally came on the scene perhaps one or two million years ago.

5. *Existing physical processes—including those related to geology, biology, and astronomy—have been acting in a consistent fashion for billions of years essentially as we see them acting in the present.* In other words, the geological, biological, and astronomical processes that we now observe in our present universe operated identically in the past at the same strength and intensity. A paleobiology professor simplifies this by saying, "because natural processes operating today have *always* operated, we can use them as a guide in understanding events throughout all geological time."[16] Therefore, the best way to understand the past is to simply observe what is happening in the present. This is a viewpoint known as uniformitarianism.[17]

Based on uniformitarianism, evolutionists calculate that the earth must be very old. They argue that because fossils seem to form rarely today, the billions of fossils that have been discovered worldwide must have taken millions of years to form.[18] Likewise, the sedimentary layers of rock are so thick (thousands of feet) that they must have taken immeasurable time to develop by ordinary processes of deposition.[19] As one evolutionist put it, "If the same rate of change had operated in the past as [is] observed in the present, it must have taken hundreds of millions of years to produce such huge thicknesses of rock and such depths of erosion."[20] Such argumentation seems persuasive— and among those persuaded by such arguments are old-earth creationists.[21]

However, young-earth creationists counter with a persuasive scenario which says that in the past, the sudden worldwide flood that came upon the earth in Noah's time upset normal geological processes on an absolutely catastrophic scale, causing mass extinction, fossilization, and layer upon layer of sedimentary rock at an unprecedented rapid rate around the world. They suggest that estimates of the earth's old age "assume that rates of sedimentation and radioactive decay have remained constant, assumptions that are impossible to verify empirically."[22] In short, they argue that what may *appear* to have taken millions of years may in reality have taken a much shorter time.

Certainly modern geologists are fully aware that such things as volcanoes and earthquakes can affect normal geological processes, prohibiting a perfect constancy in uniformitarianism.[23] But young-earth creationists believe the worldwide flood was *absolutely catastrophic,* and the effect on normal geological processes was immeasurable—much worse than any local phenomenon that has been observed in modern times. Only a worldwide catastrophic flood, they believe, can account for the sheer magnitude of geological upsets (massive volcanoes) and the vastness of mass fossil graves around the world, even atop high mountains. In this view, then, things in the past took place at enormously different rates and intensities from anything seen at present. This view obviously goes against the uniformitarianism accepted by evolutionists.

I address uniformitarianism and the fossil record in chapter 4. Now, however, I must shift attention to the critically important distinction between microevolution and macroevolution.

Microevolution vs. Macroevolution

A distinction must be made between microevolution and macroevolution, for much modern confusion on evolutionism is rooted in a confusion of these categories. Simply put, *microevolution* refers to changes that occur within the same species, while *macroevolution* refers to the transition or evolution of one species into another.[24] Macroevolution "consists of changes within a population leading to a completely new species with genetic information that did not exist in any of the parents."[25]

Creationists and evolutionists agree that microevolution has taken place. Creationists believe all the different races of human beings descended from a single common human ancestor (Adam).[26] Likewise, all kinds of dogs have "microevolved" from the original dog species created by God.[27] In no case, however, have scientists ever observed macroevolution.[28] I argue later in the book that the genetic pool of DNA in each species sets parameters beyond which the species simply cannot evolve (that is, dogs can take on new characteristics, but they cannot evolve into cats, for dog DNA always remains dog DNA, just as cat DNA always remains cat DNA).

Scripture indicates that God created the initial "kinds" of animals, and then reproduction took place, generation by generation, "according to its kind" (Genesis 1:21,24). This type of evolution is "micro" in the sense that small changes have taken place in the DNA of specific species to bring about minor changes in that species. So, for example, human DNA allows humans to have different eye colors, different hair colors, different heights, dark skin or light skin, a bulky frame or a scrawny frame, a thin body or a fat body, and so forth. The possibility for all kinds of variations such as these are encoded into the DNA of the human species.[29]

All of this contrasts with macroevolution, which, as noted previously, refers to large-scale transitions of one species into another through the process of natural selection.[30] Evolutionists believe that only the best-fit members of each species survive and transmit their genetic characteristics in increasing numbers to succeeding generations, while those less adapted are weeded out.[31] Through this "survival of the fittest" mechanism, species can allegedly evolve or transform into entirely new species. Simple life-forms can allegedly evolve or transform into more complex life-forms.

This is where the confusion often emerges in the theory of evolution. While microevolution is an observable fact, evolutionists have in the past tended to speak of evolution as a *single unitary process* (merging micro- and macroevolution into one category) such that proof for microevolution is viewed as proof for macroevolution. *This conclusion is entirely unwarranted.*[32] The extrapolation from microevolution to macroevolution is an idea rejected even by many nontheistic biologists.[33]

An illustration of this folly involves the well-known evolutionist Stephen Jay Gould, who wrote an article entitled "Evolution as Fact and Theory" in *Discovery Magazine*. In the article he emphatically stated that scientists now have "observational evidence of evolution in action." However, the examples he cites are actually examples of *micro*evolution in action, not *macro*evolution.[34] Some evolutionists try to claim that macroevolution is microevolution over a very long time (like billions of years),[35] but such a claim flies in the face of everything scientists have observed in the world of nature.

What scientific observation clearly reveals is that variations do occur within species (within fixed limits), but one species does not transition into an entirely new species. So, to cite my previous example, variations have occurred within the "dog kind," but we never witness the dog evolving into another species. Variations have occurred within the "cat kind," but we never witness the cat evolving into another species. Arguing for the validity of macroevolution based on the observation of microevolution is unscientific.

Christian scholars Norman Geisler and Joseph Holden provide this helpful chart to summarize key differences between microevolution and macroevolution[36]:

Microevolution	Macroevolution
Changes in kinds	Changes of kinds
Change within one kind of bird	Change from reptile to bird
Possible to occur	Impossible to occur
Many fossils to support	No fossil support
Does occur today	Does not occur today
Can be observed	Cannot be observed
Scientific	Unscientific

Darwin Was Aware of Problems with Evolution

Charles Darwin was certainly aware that his theory of evolution had some problems. In fact, his book *On the Origin of Species*, which is full of all kinds of observational data, catalogues key problems with his theory, admitting he simply cannot answer some questions but also suggesting possible solutions to some of the problems.[37]

For example, Darwin admitted that if his theory were true, intermediate fossils should show transitions of one species into another (macroevolution). At the time he wrote his book, no such intermediates had been discovered. Darwin suggested, however, that the fossil record was sketchy and incomplete, and he expressed hope that one day intermediates would be discovered. He also suggested that the geological conditions under which a new species might emerge in a given area were such that fossilization was not likely to occur, and therefore the fossil records may contain less evidence of intermediates.[38]

This answer served to convince many of Darwin's contemporaries of the validity of evolution. But since his day, massive numbers (billions) of fossil discoveries have proved beyond any shadow of a doubt that *no true intermediate forms exist in the fossil records*. (I address this in detail in chapter 4.)

The Persistence of Evolution

Despite the problems many have pointed out regarding evolutionary theory (I focus attention on these problems in subsequent chapters), the theory persists and will seemingly not go away. In fact, evolution now seems to permeate our culture far beyond mere biological processes. Today evolutionary theory has been applied to virtually every area of life, including the social sciences, humanities, economics, business, and politics. Evolutionist Julian Huxley said that following Darwin's discovery,

> the concept of evolution was soon extended into other than biological fields. Inorganic subjects such as the life-histories of stars and the formation of the chemical elements on the one hand, and on the other hand subjects like linguistics, social anthropology, and comparative law and religion, began to be studied from an evolutionary angle, until today we are enabled to see evolution as a universal and all-pervading process.[39]

One of the reasons why evolution is so "all-pervading" today is that the philosophy of naturalism is all-pervading. We now turn our attention to this issue.

Evolutionism Rests on the Foundation of Naturalism

Naturalism is a system of thought that espouses the idea that all phenomena in the universe can be explained wholly in terms of natural causes and laws.[1] Nature is the "whole show." No supernatural being intervenes in the natural world. Naturalists reject miracles outright.

The late famous scientist Carl Sagan, in his popular PBS television show *Cosmos*, said that "the cosmos is all that is or ever was or ever will be." More than one scholar has noted that Sagan's comment seems to be a purposeful substitution for the "Gloria Patri": "Glory be to the Father and to the Son and to the Holy Ghost. As it was in the beginning, is now, and ever shall be, world without end."[2]

Of course, Sagan did not believe in the Father and the Son and the Holy Ghost. He did not believe in the existence of a Creator. To him, the universe was infinitely old and self-existing. The universe alone gave birth to life on this planet. We are literally children of the cosmos.

Historically, in the early seventeenth century, René Descartes propagated the idea that the universe was a purely mechanical system. And because it was a purely mechanical system, it could be studied and measured. When Newtonian physics came on the scene some years later, naturalism swung into the mainstream. Scholar Del Ratzsch explains:

> Many of Newton's followers interpreted both Newton and Newtonian physics as implying (1) that nothing was truly scientific except empirical observation and what could be logically supported by those observations, and (2) that (as Descartes had argued) nature was nothing but a vast, self-regulating physical machine. Although Newton himself held neither of those positions, they were nonetheless widely believed to have the authority of both Newton and his science behind them.[3]

So, instead of believing in a transcendent Creator who brought the physical universe into being, naturalism teaches that the world of nature is a closed system of purely material causes and effects. This natural world cannot be influenced by anything outside the natural world—like God.

Today naturalism is still with us and is seemingly all-pervasive. One scholar commented that naturalism is the "air we breathe. It pervades our cultural atmosphere."[4] Naturalism virtually rules the academic world. Its presence is oppressively felt in public schools, colleges, and universities across the country. Naturalism has been called "the default position for all serious inquiry,"[5] and predominates in education, law, the arts, and of course, science. Many of today's intellectual attacks against the Bible and Christianity—and creationism—are rooted in naturalism.

In this world, where naturalism seems to reign, science is considered supreme. Through scientific observation, we learn things about the natural world. With scientific hypotheses, people speculate about causes and effects in the natural world.

In scientific language, writers describe the natural world. And, in fact, whatever conflicts with science today (like creationism) is viewed as unworthy of serious consideration.[6]

If you are getting the feeling that science today is philosophically biased, you are right on target! To be sure, science has an objective element, and this objectivity involves empirical observations, the formulation of hypotheses, the testing of those hypotheses by replication, and so forth. At the same time, however, the worldview bias that permeates the thinking of scientists in all they do, guiding their observations and their hypotheses, is naturalism.[7]

The great commandment of naturalism seems to be: "Thou shalt assume that everything in the universe has a natural explanation." And the second commandment is much like it: "Thou shalt not even ponder the possibility that anything (or anyone) outside the natural world (like God) has influenced the natural world, for this natural world is all that exists, and it is a closed system." Because scientists automatically assume naturalism is true, they will always interpret whatever they discover in terms of the "preunderstanding" of naturalism. No exceptions.

God Does Not Guide

Humanistic evolutionists are resolute in their position that evolution is an unguided, unsupervised, mindless, purposeless, impersonal process. Life on earth is nothing more than a cosmic accident. Humanist Paul Kurtz, writing several decades after the publication of the *Humanist Manifesto II,* commented:

> Naturalists maintain that there is no scientific evidence for a divine scheme of salvation, no discernible teleological purpose in nature, and that there are likewise insufficient grounds to believe in the immortality of the soul. The classical doctrine of creationism and its promise of an afterlife no doubt

express the passionate existential yearning of human
beings to transcend death. The theory of evolution,
however, provides a more parsimonious account of
human origins which is based upon evidence drawn
from a wide range of the sciences.[8]

Evolutionist Julian Huxley likewise asserted that in view of
the "proven" truth of evolution, man can "no longer take refuge
from his loneliness in the arms of a divine father figure whom
he has himself created."[9] God is viewed as a mere invention of
human culture. Those who hold on to belief in God are simply
displaying their pitiful ignorance. Appealing to the supernatural is therefore nonsensical. We are all alone in this great big
universe, and we'd better get used to dealing with our problems
on our own.

Evolutionist Stephen Jay Gould (an avowed atheist) likewise
dismissed the idea that God guides the world of nature. He
forcefully argued that no external forces propel the process of
evolution and that one simply will not find evidence for God
in the "products of nature."[10] The world of nature is a closed
system of material causes and effects and can admit no external influence.[11]

Dismissing the reality of God has the added benefit for naturalists that they have no moral accountability to a Supreme Being.
Thomas Huxley—a champion of "aggressive secular material-
ism"[12]—was personally comforted with the philosophy of naturalism and the accompanying idea that he had no God to answer
to at a future judgment. This is no doubt one of the appeals of
naturalism: freedom from the weight of moral obligation.[13]

Huxley was quite outspoken about his anti-God views.[14] A
case in point is his public debate with Anglican bishop Samuel
Wilberforce. According to Michael Behe's account, the bishop
asked, "I beg to know, is it through his grandfather or grand-
mother that Huxley claims his descent from a monkey?" Huxley

muttered, "The Lord has delivered him into my hands." Huxley then launched into his defense by giving an exposition on naturalistic biology. Behe notes that as Huxley closed his line of argument, he said that

> he didn't know whether it was through his grandmother or grandfather that he was related to an ape, but that he would rather be descended from simians [apes] than be a man possessed of the gift of reason and see it used as the bishop had used it that day. Ladies fainted, scientists cheered, and reporters ran to print the headline: "War Between Science and Theology."[15]

No Miracles

C.S. Lewis once wrote, "If you begin by ruling out the supernatural, you will perceive no miracles."[16] He was right. The philosophy of naturalism asserts that the universe operates according to uniform natural causes and that no force outside the universe can intervene in the cosmos. This is an antisupernatural assumption that prohibits any possibility of miracles.

Naturalists dismiss miracles in many ways. Some say the observers of alleged miracles are simply mistaken. Others argue that just because we don't have a present explanation for some inexplicable event does not mean the supernatural was involved; as we grow in our understanding of the natural processes, we may come to a new natural understanding regarding what many previously thought were miraculous events. Almost all critics of miracles hold that the statistical consistency of natural law (or "laws of nature") is such that supernatural events are impossible.

Sometimes we come across references to the "miracles of modern technology." Naturalists argue that if our ancestors witnessed some of the advances we have today—the space shuttle, cell phone, DVD player, computer, and the like—they would surely consider such things as miraculous. Naturalists thus reason that the more scientific understanding we have, the less we need to believe in the supernatural.

The possibility of miracles has long been denied by naturalist and humanistic thinkers. Benedict Spinoza denied the possibility of miracles because they are irrational. Rudolph Bultmann said that miracles were simply part of the mythological worldview that was part and parcel of biblical times. Immanuel Kant argued that miracles are not essential to religion.[17] But perhaps the most prolific debunker of miracles was David Hume.

Hume was a British empiricist (meaning he believed all knowledge comes from the five senses) and a skeptic of the Enlightenment. In a chapter entitled "On Miracles" in his *Enquiry Concerning Human Understanding,* he argued that, given the general experience of the uniformity of nature, miracles are highly improbable, and that the evidence in their favor is far from convincing.[18] He wrote: "A miracle is a violation of the laws of nature; and as a firm and unalterable experience has established these laws, the proof against a miracle, from the very nature of the fact, is as entire as any argument from experience can possibly be imagined."[19]

In his thinking, since all of one's knowledge is derived from experience, and since this experience conveys the absolute regularity of nature, any report of a miracle is much more likely to be a false report than a true interruption in the uniform course of nature. Hence, a report of a resurrection from the dead (for example) is in all probability a deceptive report.

Randal Keynes, the great-great-grandson of Charles Darwin, tells us that David Hume was one of Darwin's "guiding lights."[20] In keeping with Hume's guidance, Darwin "proposed an explanation for evolution that did not rely on any supernatural powers or forces. He explained evolution naturally, that is, by using phenomena and processes that everybody could daily observe in nature."[21] Darwin was "an ardent naturalist," pure and simple.[22] He jettisoned God out the back door.

Responding to Naturalism

A proper response to the philosophy of naturalism requires a book-length treatment.[23] For the purposes of this chapter, however, space allows for only a few salient points. First and foremost, naturalism can be undermined by the very science it claims to hold in high regard. As Phillip E. Johnson says, the one thing that might suffice to bring naturalism to its knees is the fact that the gap is widening between naturalism and the plain facts of scientific investigation. He suggests that "the beginning of the end will come when Darwinists are forced to face this one simple question: What should we do if empirical evidence and materialist philosophy are going in different directions?"[24]

What would one do, for example, if hard scientific evidence were discovered that proved beyond any doubt that the universe is the result of intelligent design instead of just random mechanical processes? In fact, I believe we are witnessing this discovery in our own day. In chapter 8 of this book, I examine in detail the exciting field of intelligent design theory. In my view, intelligent design may be just the thing that will punch a big hole in the boat of naturalism.

Beyond the scientific undermining of naturalism, the creationist can also intelligently respond to naturalism's rejection of the possibility of miracles (such as the miracle of creation). In what follows, I will offer four brief points in this regard.

1. *There is uniformity in the present cosmos.* Contrary to the typical evolutionist caricature, creationists do not argue against the idea of uniform "laws of nature" in the present cosmos, nor do they hold such laws in low regard. As theologian John Witmer put it,

The Christian position is not that the universe is capricious and erratic. Christians expect the sun to rise in the east tomorrow as it always has just as everyone else does. Christians recognize that this world is a cosmos, an orderly system, not a chaos. More than that, Christians agree that the regularity of the universe is observable by men and expressible in principles or laws. As a result Christians do not deny the existence of what are called the laws of nature. Nor do they think that the occurrence of miracles destroys these laws or makes them inoperative.[25]

What Christians take exception to is the notion that the universe is a self-contained, closed system with absolute laws that are *inviolable*. Christians believe that the reason for regularity in the universe—the reason we can observe "laws" in the world of nature—is that God designed creation that way. We must remember, however, that the laws of nature are merely observations of uniformity or constancy in nature. They are not forces which initiate action. They simply describe the way nature behaves when its course is not affected by a superior power. But God is not prohibited from taking action in the world if He so desires.

Scripture tells us that God is the Sustainer and Governor of the universe (Acts 14:16-17; 17:24-28). The Bible shows Jesus "upholding all things by the word of his power" (Hebrews 1:3 KJV), and "all things consist" in Him (Colossians 1:17 KJV). That which from a human vantage point is called a "law of nature" is in reality nothing more than God's normal cosmos-sustaining power at work! As Reformed scholar Louis Berkhof put it, these laws of nature are

God's usual method of working in nature. It is His good pleasure to work in an orderly way and through secondary causes. But this does not mean that He cannot depart from the established order, and cannot produce an extraordinary effect, which does not result from natural causes, by a single volition, if He deems it desirable for the end in view. When God works miracles, He produces extraordinary effects in a supernatural way.[26]

2. *Miracles do not violate the laws of nature.* If one defines a miracle as a violation of the absolute laws of nature, like David Hume did, then the possibility of miracles occurring seems slim. However, as theologian Charles Ryrie notes, a miracle does not contradict nature because "nature is not a self-contained whole; it is only a partial system within a total reality, and a miracle is consistent within that greater system which includes the supernatural."[27]

When a miracle occurs, the laws of nature are not violated but are rather superseded by a higher (supernatural) manifestation of the will of God. The forces of nature are not obliterated or suspended but are only counteracted at a particular point by a superior force.[28] As the famous physicist Sir George Stokes has said, "It may be that the event which we call a miracle was brought on not by a suspension of the laws in ordinary operation, but by the super-addition of something not ordinarily in operation."[29] In other words, miracles do not go against the regular laws of cause and effect, they simply have a cause that transcends nature.[30]

Apologists Kenneth Boa and Larry Moody explain it this way:

> Since miracles, if they occur, are empowered by something higher than nature, they must supersede the ordinary processes or laws of nature. If you took a flying leap off the edge of a sheer cliff, the phenomenon that

we call the law of gravity would surely bring you to an untimely end. But if you leaped off the same cliff in a hang glider, the results would (hopefully!) be quite different. The principle of aerodynamics in this case overcomes the pull of gravity as long as the glider is in the air. In a similar way, the occurrence of a miracle means that a higher (supernatural) principle has overcome a lower (natural) principle for the duration of the miracle. To claim that miracles violate or contradict natural laws is just as improper as to say that the principle of aerodynamics violates the law of gravity.[31]

Boa and Moody further illustrate their point with the fictional story of a Martian who lands his spacecraft atop a building in Chicago. The Martian looks over the edge of the building and observes how people respond to traffic lights. Green lights cause people to go; yellow lights cause people to slow down; red lights cause people to stop. He observes this consistent pattern for a solid hour. All the sudden, the Martian witnesses a vehicle with flashing red lights and a siren, and against all that he has thus far observed, the vehicle goes straight through the red light. "'Aha!' he said, 'there must be a higher law! When you have a flashing light and a loud sound, you can go through the crossing regardless of what color the light may be.'"[32]

This little story illustrates that the natural laws of the universe can be (and are on occasion) overruled by a higher law. The universe is not a closed system that prevents God from breaking in with the miraculous. God does not violate the laws of nature but rather supersedes them with a higher law. God is over, above, and outside natural law and is not bound by it.

Scientists may claim that such miracles would disrupt any possibility of doing real science by removing constancy in the world. But constancy is in the world because God created the world that way. Miracles are unusual events that involve only a brief superseding of the natural laws. By definition, they are out of the norm. If a norm did not exist, miracles would not be possible. As apologists Peter Kreeft and Ronald Tacelli put it, "Unless there are regularities, there can be no exceptions to them."[33] Miracles are unusual, not commonplace events. A miracle is a unique event that stands out against the background of ordinary and regular occurrences. The possibility of miracles does not disrupt the possibility of doing real science because God has built constancy into the universe via the laws of nature.

3. *David Hume's experience was greatly limited.* As noted previously, Hume argued that a "miracle is a violation of the laws of nature; and as a firm and unalterable experience has established these laws, the proof against a miracle, from the very nature of the fact, is as entire as any argument from experience can possibly be imagined."[34]

The big problem with Hume's conclusion is that "experience" can never confirm his naturalistic viewpoint unless he has access to all possible experiences in the universe, including those of the past and the future. Since (finite) Hume does not have access to this much broader (infinite) body of knowledge, his conclusion is baseless.[35]

The reality is that we could trust very little history if we were to believe only those things which we have personally observed and experienced! Sadly, though, this is the methodology modernistic critics still hold onto regarding miracles.

Apologists Norman L. Geisler and Ronald M. Brooks have noted that Hume essentially equates *probability* with *evidence*. Since people who die typically stay dead, a so-called miracle of resurrection is impossible. Geisler and Brooks counter, "That is like saying that you shouldn't believe it if you won the lottery because of all the thousands of people who lost. It equates evidence with probability and says that you should never believe that long shots win."[36] A miracle may be a "long shot," and it may not happen very often, but long shots make good sense when God is involved in the picture. What is impossible with man is possible with God (Matthew 19:26).

4. *If God exists, then miracles are possible.* The bottom line, once you get rid of all the fancy philosophical arguments against miracles, is this: If one admits God may exist, miracles are possible. Paul Little writes, "Once we assume the existence of God, there is no problem with miracles, because God is by definition all-powerful."[37] Reformed scholar Charles Hodge, in his *Systematic Theology*, similarly writes: "If theism [belief in a personal Creator-God] be once admitted, then it must be admitted that the whole universe, with all that it contains and all the laws by which it is controlled, must be subject to the will of God."[38] As Norman Geisler put it so well, "If there is a God who can *act*, then there can be *acts* of God. The only way to show that miracles are impossible is to disprove the existence of God."[39] And that is something that naturalists cannot do![40]

What does all this mean for our present study? It means that the assumptions that undergird naturalism—such as the idea that the natural world is a closed system, the idea that we have no God who can intervene, the idea that we can account for all things in the universe by materialistic causes and effects, and so forth—are false assumptions. And since naturalism undergirds evolution, evolution too finds its foundational base collapsing.

Later in the book, I demonstrate substantial evidence that a transcendent and powerful God—an intelligent Designer—created the universe and left His fingerprints all over it.[41] This evidence, many believe, deals a philosophical deathblow to naturalism.

Christians Have Diverse Views

A book like this would be easier to write if all Christians uniformly believed the same thing on the issue of man's origin. But they do not.[1] All Christians believe in God, but they hold to a variety of interpretations regarding His role in man's origin.

Among the views Christians have held on this issue are the gap theory, progressive creationism, theistic evolution, and young-earth creationism. A basic working knowledge of these diverse viewpoints will help you understand the creation-evolution debate. In what follows, then, I will present summaries of each position followed by objections raised against them.

The Gap Theory

The gap theory teaches that God created the world perhaps billions of years ago, and it was perfect and beautiful in every way. This is the creation described in Genesis 1:1. This creation was populated with plants and animals and perhaps even with a race of pre-Adamic men who had no souls. Then, as a result of Lucifer's rebellion and fall (Isaiah 14; Ezekiel 28), the earth— Lucifer's domain—became chaos. The picture of formlessness, emptiness, and darkness in Genesis 1:2 is allegedly a picture of divine judgment, for God could not have originally created the earth this way (see Isaiah 24:1; 45:18; Jeremiah 4:23-26).[2] Darkness is often used as a symbol of judgment and sin in Scripture (John 3:19; Jude 13). The original creation in Genesis 1:1 was one of light, but after God judged the earth, it was characterized by darkness (verse 2). Millions of years—perhaps even billions of years—are said to have taken place between verses 1 and 2.[3] Hence the "gap" theory.

Gap proponents typically translate Genesis 1:2 this way: "But the earth *became* without form and empty" (italics added). Traditional translations render it, "But the earth *was* without form and empty" (italics added). Gap proponents argue that the earth "became" (Hebrew: *hayetha*) without form and empty when God judged the world as a result of Lucifer's sin. The words "without form and void" (Hebrew: *tohu wa-bohu*) appear elsewhere only in Isaiah 34:11 and Jeremiah 4:23, and in these verses "formless" and "void" speak of judgment and destruction. Therefore, the words must have the same meaning in Genesis 1:2.

In this view, God's judgment on the earth involved a devastating global flood followed by an Ice Age. All life on planet earth was apparently extinguished. The apparent old age of the earth and the extensive fossils showing development over long periods of time relate to this first creation.[4] The six days of creation discussed throughout the rest of Genesis 1 (verse 2 and following) relate to God's *re*-creation or restoration of the earth, not the original creation.[5] This reconstruction probably took place around 4000 B.C.

The gap theory has been held by such notable scholars as John Eadie, F. Delitzsch, Arthur Custance, C.I. Scofield (of the famous *Scofield Study Bible*), G.H. Pember, Arthur W. Pink, and Donald Grey Barnhouse. Out of all the "gap" proponents I have read, Barnhouse's explanation is the most lucid. Following are a few distinctive highlights of his version:

Barnhouse argues that one of the big mistakes Christians make in Bible interpretation is that they have a tendency to see the events in Genesis 1:1 as closely connected in time to verse 2. He argues for a great gulf (or "gap") between the two, perhaps involving millions of years.[6]

The first creation was perfect. Barnhouse makes much of Isaiah 45:18 in support of the theory. This verse reads, "For this is what the Lord says—he who created the heavens, he is God; he who fashioned and made the earth, he founded it; *he did not create it to be empty, but formed it to be inhabited*" (italics added). Clearly, God did not create the original earth as "empty." The original creation was perfect in every way.

Barnhouse says that following the original perfect creation, God placed a magnificent being on the earth to govern it, and his name was Lucifer. But after a time, this magnificent being rebelled against God and sought to take God's place. God was therefore forced to judge his domain, planet earth.

> That something tremendous and terrible happened to the first, perfect creation is certain…. Somewhere back before the chaos of the second verse of Genesis there is a great tragedy and a terrible catastrophe…. We know that it was the hand of a holy God which struck the earth into ruin because of a great outbreak of rebellion.[7]

Barnhouse then explains the gap:

> The judgment of God on Satan's rebellion turned out the lights on this world. We do not know how long this period of judgment lasted. It may have been long ages. The geologists tell us of the scars of the travail of earlier years, and they believe that millions of years must have been necessary to have brought about some

of the phenomena which are found in the earth. Let
it be millions of years. Whatever the theory as to
primeval time, it can be dropped into the vastness of
Genesis.[8]

Lucifer thus witnessed his domain demolished. He could do
nothing to prevent it. Lucifer sinned against God, and God
blasted the earth in judgment. At this time, "the earth became
without form and void, a wreck and a ruin, a chaos, and darkness was upon the face of the deep." Later, "on the occasion of
the creation of Adam, God moved to re-form, to refashion, this
earth."[9]

Objections to the Gap Theory

The gap theory sounds like a great story! It is full of interesting drama. However, many biblical scholars have raised serious objections to the theory.

1. The grammar of Genesis 1:1-2 does not allow for a gap.
Verse one is an independent clause. Verse two is composed of
three circumstantial clauses (that is, clauses that explain the
"circumstances" of the earth when God began to create). No
grammatical break exists between verses 1 and 2. Further,
Genesis 1 provides no context of judgment.

2. Genesis 3:17-19 indicates that *Adam's* fall, not Satan's,
resulted in the judgment of the earth. God said to Adam,
"Cursed is the ground because of you; through painful toil you
will eat of it all the days of your life. It will produce thorns and
thistles for you, and you will eat the plants of the field."

3. The gap theory depends on the phrase "formless and void"
meaning "evil" or "the result of judgment." Such a conclusion
is unwarranted. Notice that the usage of the Hebrew word *tohu*
(emptiness) in Job 26:7 does not support the idea of intrinsic
judgment: "He [God] spreads out the northern [skies] over *empty*

space; he suspends the earth over nothing." (Space can be utterly empty without being evil!)

In the same way, the use of *tohu* (emptiness) in Isaiah 45:18 does not connote judgment: "For this is what the LORD says— he who created the heavens, he is God; he who fashioned and made the earth, he founded it; he did not create it to be *empty*, but formed it to be inhabited." This verse is perfectly compatible with the traditional understanding of creation. That is, God first created the "stuff" of the earth, and then molded it into shape so it could be inhabited. Just as a potter first gets a glob of clay and then molds it into shape, so God created a "glob" of (empty) earth material and then molded it into a beautiful planet, fit for habitation.

4. The argument that Genesis 1:2 should be translated "the earth *became* without form and empty" is unwarranted. The Hebrew word *hayetha* can be translated this way, but this usage is rare in the Old Testament, and *hayetha* should not be translated this way without compelling evidence to do so. Only 22 occasions out of 1522 usages of the word in the Old Testament use this translation.[10] In the Pentateuch (the first five books of the Bible), *hayetha* is translated "was" in 258 out of 264 instances.[11] Clearly, the word should usually be translated as "was." All of the standard translations of the Bible render Genesis 1:2, "the earth *was* without form and empty."

5. The argument that the presence of darkness in Genesis 1:2 ("darkness was over the surface of the deep") necessarily indicates sin and judgment is not persuasive. For example, Psalm 104:20 says of God: "You bring darkness, it becomes night, and all the beasts of the forest prowl." This verse has no hint of darkness being evil. Context always determines how the word *darkness* should be understood, and Genesis 1 has no hint of sin or judgment.

6. If the gap theory were correct, then God's estimate of the created earth as being "very good" (Genesis 1:31) would not

make much sense. After all, Adam would have been walking on an earth in which untold numbers of animals and perhaps pre-Adamites had died and been buried. As John Whitcomb notes, Adam would have been walking upon a graveyard of billions of creatures.[12] And this earth would have already been the judged domain of the fallen Lucifer. All this hardly seems "very good."

7. Scripture plainly states that God created *everything* in six days. In Exodus 20:11 we read, "For in six days the LORD made the heavens and the earth, the sea, and *all that is in them,* but he rested on the seventh day. Therefore the LORD blessed the Sabbath day and made it holy" (italics added). Since *everything* the Lord created was done in six days, that leaves no room for God to have engaged in a previous creation.

Progressive Creationism

Progressive creationism is the idea that God created directly and deliberately via a series of creative acts over very long periods of time. The "days" of Genesis are not consecutive twenty-four-hour days but are ages or epochs, or perhaps literal days that marked only the beginning of successive long creative periods.[13] Some of these various creative periods may have overlapped with each other to a certain degree.[14] This view has been held by such well-known Christians as Eric Sauer (author of *King of the Earth*), Davis Young (author of *Creation and the Flood: An Alternative to Flood Geology*), and Reformed scholar James Boice.

According to progressive creationism, life on earth could not have emerged without intelligent intervention. This view rejects that idea that macroevolution can account for "the increasing complexity and relatively abrupt appearance of new life-forms in the fossil record." They propose that "the scientific evidence is more compatible with the hypothesis that God acted miraculously several times throughout biological history."[15]

Progressive creationists typically argue that God created the first member of each "kind," and from that first kind others developed via evolution. They are careful to note that they accept only microevolution (evolution within species).[16] As theologian Millard Erickson explains it, "God may have created the first member of the cat family. From it developed lions, tigers, leopards, and just plain pussycats."[17] God would then create another "kind" (such as dogs), and from this first creation many varieties evolved. God would later create perhaps a horse "kind," and from that would evolve all kinds of different horses. One progressive creationist gives this explanation: "We think God's activity in creation occurred in a progression—a number of steps over a long period of time."[18]

When God finally decided to create man, God created him directly and completely. God did not take a creature that already existed (some kind of prehuman life-form) and then mold him into a human. Rather, God created him "from the ground up" both physically and spiritually. (As we will see, this serves to distinguish progressive creationism from theistic evolution.)

This means that God interspersed several special acts of creation at strategic points throughout a long evolutionary process.[19] Those who hold to this viewpoint are able to say that they believe in creationism, but they're also able to say they believe in evolution—at least to a degree.

Progressive creationists are open about the fact that they have a high view of science. They are generally willing to reinterpret Scripture if some new scientific discovery makes a previous understanding of Scripture untenable. So, for example, in view of the apparent antiquity of the earth, they interpret Scripture in a way that allows for a long period of creation, turning the "days" of Genesis into long periods.[20] Progressive creationists suggest, "Ultimately, responsible geology must determine the length of the Genesis days, even as science centuries earlier settled the issue of the rotation of the earth about the sun."[21] They say that "in this sort of scheme, we can get a very nice correlation between the creation account in Genesis and a reasonable model for the earth's origin as commonly proposed by astronomy and geology."[22]

Progressive creationists find theological support for the idea that the "days" in Genesis are long periods of time. For example, in Genesis 2:4 (KJV), *day* refers to the entire time frame during which God created. In Job 20:28, "day" refers to the time of God's wrath. In Psalm 20:1 (KJV), "day" refers to a time of trouble. Moreover, in 2 Peter 3:8 we are told, "With the Lord a day is like a thousand years, and a thousand years are like a day" (see also Psalm 90:4). Gordon R. Lewis and Bruce A. Demarest argue that *yom*, the Hebrew word for *day*, can be translated as "time," "year," and "age," among other meanings, and therefore can lexically refer to a long period of time.[23] In addition, the sun was not created until the fourth day of creation, so the first three days certainly couldn't have been literal twenty-four-hour "solar" days. Also, God "rested" on the seventh day (Genesis 2:2), and since that rest *continues even to the present today* (Hebrews 4:3), the seventh day must involve a long period of time (and so *all seven* days must be ages). Still further, the events that took place during the sixth day of creation would have taken far longer than a single twenty-four-hour day.[24] (For example, Adam's naming of the animals must have taken more than one day.)

Progressive creationists recognize that the genealogies contained in Genesis seem to prohibit long ages. However, they argue that genealogies in the Bible often had gaps in them, and therefore more time is allowed for than a strict literal reading of Genesis would seem to indicate.

Typically, they deny that the flood of Noah's day was a universal flood, opting instead for a local flood confined to the Mesopotamian area. They argue that the Bible sometimes employs universal terms when, in fact, only a limited meaning is possible (see for example, Genesis 41:57; Deuteronomy 2:25; 1 Kings 18:10; Psalm 22:17; Matthew 3:5; John 4:39). "The universality of the flood may simply mean the universality of experience of those who reported it."[25]

Objections to Progressive Creationism

1. Progressive creationists have found themselves on the receiving end of strong criticism from both young-earth creationists and evolutionists. Evolutionists, for example, say that this theory is simply postulating a "God of the gaps"—that is, progressive creationists appeal to God as Creator of a new species whenever the fossil records have a notable gap. God allegedly steps in from time to time during the process of evolution to create new life-forms. Evolutionists resist running to God every time we find scientific difficulties in the fossils. Otherwise, true science will never get done. By invoking supernatural explanations when natural explanations fail, progressive creationism leads to a stifling of scientific progress.[26]

2. Young-earth creationists focus much of their criticism on the "day-age" theory—the idea that the "days" in Genesis 1 are actually long periods of time. They point out that the Genesis account makes reference to evening and morning, indicating that literal days are meant (Genesis 1:5).[27] Professor Charles Ryrie writes:

> The qualifying phrase "evening and morning" attached to each of the six days of Creation supports the meaning of the days as twenty-four-hour periods. Proponents of the day-age idea reply that evening and morning is a figure of speech for beginning and ending. Each "evening" saw the completion of the work of that age which was followed by the "morning" of renewed activity. But evening and morning, each occurring more

than 100 times in the Old Testament, are never used
to mean anything other than a literal evening and literal
morning, ending or beginning a solar day.[28]

3. We read in Genesis that God created the sun to rule the
day and the moon to rule the night. This would seem to indicate that the "days" were literal solar days (Genesis 1:16).

4. Solar days seem to be implied in Exodus 20:11, where
we are told that "in six days the LORD made the heavens and
the earth, the sea, and all that is in them, but he rested on the
seventh day."

5. Whenever a number is used with the Hebrew word for
"day" *(yom),* it always refers to a literal solar day (no exceptions
in the Old Testament). Since God is said to have created the
universe in "six days," literal solar days must be meant.[29]

6. If Genesis had intended to communicate that God created
during long periods, there was a perfectly acceptable Hebrew
word that would have been ideal to communicate this
concept: *olam.*[30] But this word is not used. *Yom* is used, and as
noted above, *yom* with a number always refers to a twenty-four-
hour day.

7. Even though 2 Peter 3:8 says, "With the Lord a day is
like a thousand years, and a thousand years are like a day," this
does not give support to the idea that the "days" in Genesis are
periods of time. The verse does not indicate that a day for God
actually *lasts* a thousand years. Rather it says that a day is *like*
a thousand years. John Whitcomb suggests that this verse indicates that "God is above the limitations of time in the sense
that he can accomplish in one literal day what nature or man
could not accomplish in a vast period of time, if ever."[31]

8. The progressive creationist objection that Adam, during
the sixth day, could not have done what he is reported to have
done in a twenty-four-hour day (such as naming the animals)
is not persuasive. Creationist Henry Morris notes that the

"kinds" created by God were likely broader categories than our modern "species." We are not told how many "kinds" were involved, but Morris suggests the number was probably less than a thousand.[32]

Another factor to keep in mind is that Adam was a newly created human being who was not subject to the debilitating effects of the fall and God's judgment. Medical specialists today tell us that human beings presently use only a small percentage of the brain. Adam, freshly created by God, may well have had 100 percent mental capacity, so the task at hand would not have been nearly as challenging for him as it would be for us today. Further, since Adam was newly created as an adult, God would have had to instill in Adam's brain a perfect human language that Adam would have easily used to accomplish his task.[33]

9. The Genesis account indicates that God created Adam on day six, and Adam lived on through day seven and continued to live in the days that followed. If the days of Genesis were in fact long ages, how can we reconcile these many thousands of years with the biblical statement that Adam died at age 930 (Genesis 5:5)?

10. The progressive creationist argument that the seventh day is still going on today (with God continuing to rest) is not convincing. Exodus 20:10-11 tells us that the Sabbath day for the Jews was a literal twenty-four-hour period, and this was patterned after God's (single) day of rest following the creation. Citing Hebrews 4:3-4 does not help the progressive creationist case, for this passage affirms that God "rested" (past tense) on the seventh day.[34]

11. The progressive creationist argument that the first three days could not have been literal days because the sun was not created until day four is not convincing. Indeed, young-earth creationists believe the first three days were the same length of time as the last four days. They point out that exactly the

same kinds of descriptive words are used to describe *all* the days—words like *evening* and *morning*. Some believe God created a temporary localized source of light in heaven (see Genesis 1:3) which, as the earth rotated, gave the appearance of light for the day and darkness for the night, all within a twenty-four-hour period.[35]

12. As for the progressive creationist view that the flood of Noah's day was only a local flood, the evidence points to a universal flood. The waters climbed so high on the earth that "all the high mountains under the entire heavens were covered" (Genesis 7:19). They rose so greatly on the earth that they "covered the mountains to a depth of more than twenty feet" (verse 20). The flood lasted some 377 days (nearly 54 weeks), indicating more than just local flooding.

The Bible also says that every living thing that moved on the earth perished, "*all* the creatures that swarm over the earth, and all mankind. *Everything* on dry land that had the breath of life in its nostrils died. *Every living thing* on the face of the earth was wiped out.... *Only* Noah was left, and those with him in the ark" (verses 21-23, italics added).

The language of Genesis 6–9 seems to be that of a universal flood. Furthermore, the universal view best explains the worldwide distribution of diluvian deposits. A universal flood would also explain the sudden death of many woolly mammoths frozen in Alaskan and Siberian ice. Investigation shows that these animals died suddenly by choking or drowning and not by freezing.

Still further, following this flood, God promised never to destroy humankind by such a flood again (Genesis 8:21; 9:11,15). If the flood of Noah's time was only a local flood, then God has broken His promise, for innumerable human beings have been killed in multiple local floods. But another universal flood has never occurred.

One must also wonder why Noah would spend 120 years building an ark at God's command for a local flood. Why wouldn't God just instruct him to pack up his family, get two of each of the animals, and go on a trek to a safe part of the world?

Finally, many universal flood legends (over 270) exist among people of various religions and cultural backgrounds all over the world. These people attribute the descent of all races to Noah.

Theistic Evolution

Theistic evolutionists claim the Bible teaches that God created the world and humanity, but it does not tell us *how* He did it.[36] Mixing their interpretation of Scripture with what they consider to be scientific evidence for evolution, theistic evolutionists conclude that God initially began creation, and then He directed and controlled the processes of naturalistic evolution to produce the universe as we know it today.[37] God acted as a kind of "impersonal life force inherent in the system."[38] He allegedly entered into the process of time on occasion to modify what was developing. "God created the biological world, including all past and present life-forms, by using evolutionary mechanisms."[39] Most theistic evolutionists hold to the day-age theory, though some believe the "days" in Genesis are "revelatory days" when God gave revelation about the creation. One theistic evolutionist argues that

> accepting macroevolutionism as a scientific theory does not endanger essential religious beliefs. Some evolutionary creationists interpret the biblical creation story as "days of proclamation" at the beginning of time, when God planned and proclaimed creative intent—intentions carried out via the very natural mechanisms God designed. Most evolutionary creationists see

Genesis 1 as an example of God communicating
universal, eternal truths through the limited knowledge
and cultural images of the human author.[40]

Theistic evolutionists typically deny the historicity of Adam
and Eve (as direct creations of God) in the book of Genesis.
They generally argue that at some point in the process of evolution, God took an already-existing higher primate (an ape),
modified it, put a soul within it, and transformed it into Adam,
in the "image of God." (God also transformed an existing female
higher primate into Eve.) In this view, then, God directly created
the spiritual nature of humanity, but the physical nature was a
product of evolution.

Theistic evolutionists recognize that this seems to disagree
with the statement in Genesis 2:7 that God created Adam from
the dust of the ground, so they reinterpret "dust of the ground"
metaphorically to refer to previously existing animals. By taking
a nonliteral approach to Genesis, theistic evolutionists are able
to fit their evolutionist views into it.

Objections to Theistic Evolution

1. Evolutionists and creationists rarely agree on anything,
but most seem to agree that theistic evolution is an ill-informed
position regarding man's origins. Evolutionists do not like the
theory because they do not want to allow for God or the supernatural at any point in their theory (see chapter 2, "Evolutionism Rests On the Foundation of Naturalism"). As Charles
Darwin put it, "I would give absolutely nothing for the theory
of natural selection if it requires miraculous additions at any
one stage of descent."[41]

2. Creationists point to a number of serious theological problems with theistic evolution. For one thing, it must make a
complete allegory out of Genesis 1:1–2:3, for which there is
no warrant. Nothing in Genesis indicates it is to be taken as

anything less than historical. If we start taking the approach that we can simply allegorize any portion of Scripture that doesn't agree with some aspect of modern science, we will not have much of a literal Bible left.

3. The suggestion that humanity is derived from a nonhuman ancestor cannot be reconciled with a correct understanding of Genesis 2:7: "The LORD God formed the man from the dust of the ground and breathed into his nostrils the breath of life, and the man became a living being." Notice that God created Adam's material nature from the dust of the ground. This indicates that God formed Adam from inorganic material rather than obtaining it from some previously living form (like an ape). God then created Adam's immaterial nature (the breath of life).[42]

Many scholars have noted the significance of God creating Adam as a "living being" in Genesis 2:7. The Hebrew words translated "living being" (Hebrew: *nephesh chayah*) are exactly the same words used to describe the other creatures God previously created (see Genesis 1:20,21,24). Genesis 2:7 indicates that Adam *became* a living being just as other beasts *became* living beings. In other words, Adam was not a living being until the moment he was created as one; he did not exist previously as a higher primate. Until God breathed the breath of life into Adam, he was just inanimate, lifeless matter (dust of the ground).

Further, the idea that "dust of the ground" metaphorically refers to animals is not persuasive. Consider the fact that God later informs Adam what would happen to him when he dies: "For dust you are and to dust you will return" (Genesis 3:19). If "dust of the earth" refers to animals, then we must interpret this verse to mean that when Adam dies, he returns to an animal form, a conclusion no one would agree with.[43]

4. Christ's comment about Adam and Eve's creation is particularly worthy of note (Matthew 19:4). Christ, as God, is all-knowing. Christ, as God, is also the creator of the universe (see

John 1:3; Colossians 1:16; Hebrews 1:2,10). Jesus the Creator affirmed that Adam was created not only in the image and likeness of God (spiritually) but also male and female (physically). This affirmation from Christ would be quite misleading if in fact the physical nature of man were actually derived from evolution (that is, a higher primate that was "modified"). If Christ's words cannot be trusted in these particulars about Adam, how can anyone be sure His words can be trusted in other matters?[44]

5. To simply deny the historicity of Adam is to call into question the salvific work of the "last Adam" (Jesus Christ) (see Romans 5:12-21; 1 Corinthians 15:22,45-49). If Adam never existed and fell into sin, then what need do we have for a last Adam (the Savior) to die on the cross for us?

6. Young-earth creationists criticize theistic evolution as violating a key New Testament teaching in 1 Corinthians 11:8,12: "For man did not come from woman, but woman from man.... For as woman came from man, so also man is born of woman." The apostle Paul here teaches that while men today are born of women, women had their first origin in man. The theistic evolutionist idea that woman came from a female higher primate, as man came from a male higher primate, is incompatible with this teaching.[45]

7. The apostle Paul teaches in 1 Corinthians 15:39 that "all flesh is not the same: Men have one kind of flesh, animals have another, birds another and fish another." Man was not created from an ape. Rather, humans and apes have an entirely different "flesh." This verse cannot be made to agree with theistic evolution.

8. One must ask why God would use mutations—which are generally harmful to the creature—as His means of bringing various species into being. As one scholar put it, "Why should the omniscient God, who knows precisely what He wants, set nature groping her way forward as if she were blind, to find the

path of least resistance? Why should the omnipotent God choose such a wasteful and cruel method to 'create' life?"[46]

9. Young-earth creationists also bring up the issue of death before the fall. They argue that Scripture asserts sin and death did not exist before the fall (Romans 5:12-14). If theistic evolution is correct, this would mean death and suffering existed for a long time prior to the time Adam ever came on the scene. This is unacceptable to those who read Genesis in a straightforward, literal fashion.

Young-Earth Creationism

Young-earth creationism holds that the universe was created—mature and fully functioning—during six literal days 10,000 or fewer years ago.[47] This view is held by Henry Morris, John Whitcomb, A.E. Wilder Smith, Weston Fields, John Klotz, Robert Kofahl, Kelly Segraves, and many others.[48]

Young-earth creationism disagrees with evolution and theistic evolution in that it denies that macroevolution (evolution of one species into another) had anything to do with origins. It disagrees with progressive creationism by affirming that the days of Genesis were not long periods of time but literal twenty-four-hour days.

This view holds that when God engaged in the work of creation, He did so instantaneously. Psalm 33 tells us, "By the word of the LORD were the heavens made, their starry host by the breath of his mouth.... For he spoke, and it came to be; he commanded, and it stood firm" (verses 6,9; compare with Genesis 1:3,6,9,14,20,24). Hebrews 11:3 likewise tells us that "the universe was formed at God's command." No time interval lapsed between God's commanding words and creation leaping into existence. No slow process of evolution was involved in any way.

Genesis uses three Hebrew words to describe God's work of creation. These are *bara* ("to create"), *asah* ("to make"), and *yatsar* ("to form"). God alone was responsible for creating, making, and forming all that is in the universe. And He did so without using preexisting materials. One moment, nothing existed anywhere in the universe. The next moment, after God gave the command, the universe leaped into existence. This is known among theologians as *creatio ex nihilo* (creation out of nothing). Instantaneously, God brought forth each "kind" of animal and plant, and each then reproduced "after its kind."

This reproduction "after its kind" is consistent with what we learn in 1 Corinthians 15:39 (KJV): "All flesh is not the same flesh: but there is one kind of flesh of man, another flesh of beasts, another of fishes, and another of birds." The Hebrew word for "kind" *(min)* is probably more flexible than our present "species,"[49] but the word prohibits macroevolution—the idea that one "kind" can evolve into another. Humans always reproduce as humans, dogs always reproduce as dogs, and cats always reproduce as cats. Reproducing "after its kind" does, however, allow for microevolution, involving minor changes within species. As Duane Gish points out, "each kind was created with sufficient genetic potential, or gene pool, to give rise to all the varieties within that kind that have existed in the past and those that are yet in existence today."[50]

Young-earth creationism is the viewpoint that most consistently interprets the Genesis account in a plain, straightforward, literal fashion. Sometimes young-earth creationists are caricatured as wooden literalists, but this is an unfair charge. Young-earth creationists do not hold to a wooden literalism—the kind that interprets biblical figures of speech literally. They believe that what is understood to be symbolic and what is taken literally should be based on the biblical context itself. For example, Jesus used obviously figurative parables to communicate spiritual truth.

A literal approach to Scripture recognizes that the Bible contains a variety of literary genres, and each has certain peculiar characteristics that must be recognized in order to interpret the text properly. Biblical genres include history (Acts), the dramatic epic (Job), poetry (Psalms), wise sayings (Proverbs), apocalyptic writings (Revelation), and many others. An incorrect genre judgment will lead one far astray in interpreting Scripture.

Even though the Bible contains a variety of literary genres and many figures of speech, the biblical authors most often conveyed their ideas literally. And where they express their ideas literally, the Bible expositor must explain these ideas literally. Such an approach gives to each word the same basic meaning it would have in normal, ordinary, customary usage in writing, speaking, or thinking. Without such a method, communication between God and humankind is impossible.

Young-earth creationists believe the text of Genesis indicates that it is to be taken as a historical genre. They see no marks of poetry or saga or myth in the Genesis account. They reject the method of those who believe the text of Scripture must be demythologized to make it fit with science. If we take such an approach with Genesis, what is to prevent us from interpreting any other part of Scripture in the same way? What should we do with the incarnation? The resurrection of Christ? Certainly these do not make sense according to modern science, so should they be demythologized? Young-earth creationists think not. Better to take God at His word than to succumb to a doctrinal compromise that will lead us far astray.

A young-earth creationist understanding of Genesis has been the predominant viewpoint of Christians throughout church history. Does that automatically make it the correct position? No, it doesn't. But young-earth creationists point out that Christians should be cautious about so easily dismissing what has been held to be true by Christians for two thousand years.[51]

Young-earth creationists realize that most modern scientists hold to an extremely old earth, and they realize that many interpret the fossil evidence as indicating life has been on earth for millions of years. They respond by suggesting that when God created the physical universe, He created it—and all within it—with an appearance of age.[52] Adam and Eve were certainly created as full-grown adults. We know this to be true because, among other indications, they were commanded by God to be fruitful and multiply (indicating their adult sexual maturity). They had the appearance of age even though they did not have genuine age.[53] Likewise, one must assume that a fully functioning ecosystem in the Garden of Eden would include mature trees (that had ready-to-eat fruit), bushes, and the like. Such items would have the appearance of age despite being only minutes old.[54]

This is similar to some of the miracles Christ performed during His three-year ministry on earth. For example, at a wedding banquet in Galilee, Jesus had some servants fill six stone water jars—each holding 20 to 30 gallons—and He turned the water (over 120 gallons) into wine (John 2:1-11). This miracle disclosed Jesus' power over the chemical processes of nature.[55] By a single word of command He accomplished the transformation that a vine requires several months to produce.

Shortly thereafter, Jesus multiplied five small loaves of bread and two small fish into enough food to satisfy over 5000 people. Matthew's Gospel indicates that those who partook of the food provided by Jesus included 5000 men—to say nothing of women and children (Matthew 14:21). Using a small boy's lunch, which one of the disciples located, Jesus multiplied the meager serving of unleavened barley cakes and pickled fish until everyone in the vast crowd was more than satisfied.[56] Notice that the fish served to the people were full-grown fish, with the appearance of having been in the lake for quite some time. The bread existed despite the fact that grains had not been harvested for it, nor had it gone through the process of baking.[57]

In the same way, the miracle of creation may have involved apparent age in the universe. Some, such as John Whitcomb and Henry Morris, have suggested that this "apparent age" principle might apply to radioactive substances, "meaning that such material might well have been created complete with decay products, which would completely invalidate radiometric dating (such as carbon dating)."[58]

The apparent age hypothesis is also applied to stars and the light in transit from those stars to planet earth. Of course, old-earthers would say that if the light from the star had to travel a million light-years to get to earth, then the star is at least a million years old. Young-earthers, who posit a younger dating of the universe, traditionally argue that God not only created the star but also created the light in transit from the star to planet earth.[59] In this scenario, then, the star's existence is compatible with young-earth creationism.

Objections to Young-Earth Creationism

1. Old-earth creationists raise an objection to the idea that God created light in transit from the star to planet earth. If a star is a million light-years away, and an observer on earth is looking at the star, then that observer is actually seeing what that star was like a million years ago. Therefore, observers are witnessing a "fiction."

This objection has caused some young-earth creationists to abandon the "light in transit" theory. They are presently examining other possible scientific explanations that may be compatible with their view.

2. Many have suggested that the "apparent age" hypothesis would mean that God was being deceitful.[60] To indicate that the universe was one age when in fact it is another age is not an honest thing to do—especially for a holy God.

3. The fossil evidence indicates life has been on earth for millions of years.[61] Empirical observation indicates that fossils form rarely, so the billions of fossils on earth must have taken millions of years to form. Likewise, the layers of sedimentary

rock, which are thousands of feet thick, must have taken millions of years to form.

Related to this, geologists believe that what we see around the world—fossils, volcanoes, mountains, and the like—can best be explained on the basis of the scientific theory of uniformitarianism.[62] As we saw in chapter 1, this involves the idea that the geological, biological, and astronomical processes that we now observe in our present universe operated identically in the past at the same strength and intensity. If this is correct, millions of years would have been necessary to produce the fossils, volcanoes, and mountains we see around the world.

4. Old-earth creationists (such as progressive creationists) argue against the young-earth view by pointing out that the Hebrew word for "day" *(yom)* can lexically mean "period," "epoch," or "age." Therefore, the "days" of Genesis need not be literal twenty-four-hour days. (See "Progressive Creationism," pages 50–53.)

A Young-Earth Creationist Rejoinder

Because these objections to young-earth creationism have generated considerable controversy and have entered the public arena via popular magazines and newspapers, I would be remiss if I failed to mention how young-earth creationists are responding. They are quick to respond, for example, to the allegation that the "apparent age" theory would make God dishonest. They argue that God gave humanity a book (actually, a bunch of books combined into one) called the Bible wherein He fully explained all about creation. And a plain reading of the Genesis account seems clearly to set limits on how old the earth could be. No one would suggest, they argue, that God was being deceitful to Adam when He presented a full-grown Eve to him. No one would suggest that Jesus was deceiving the wedding guests when the water He had turned into wine was served to them.

One scholar has noted that rocks and fossils do not come with a date stamp on them. Rather, scientists devise theories to postulate age. If the universe is in fact young, why should God be blamed simply because our scientific method was inaccurate? "Do we presume that our theories are so good that we are correctly interpreting what the rocks and fossils actually say— so that if they do not mean what we think they say about their age, then their Creator is responsible for their prevarication?"[63]

As for the objection that fossil evidence supports an old earth, young-earth creationists reply that the only sufficient explanation for all the various strata formation, fossil remains around the world, massive volcanic activity, and mountain formation is a universal catastrophic Noachian flood that lasted a full year. The waves of this flood would have swept up all forms of life, and the mud into which these various forms of life finally settled solidified into rock as a result of the tremendous pressure of the water. Because the flood produced wave after wave after wave, layers of rock strata eventually formed, full of fossils of dead animals and plants. What normally would have taken immeasurable time to occur (millions of years) took place in a relatively short time as a result of the catastrophic flood. Fossilization of whole organisms in sedimentary rocks must have taken place rapidly (as would necessarily be the case in a catastrophic flood) because otherwise, in normal conditions, not much of the organism would be left to fossilize after decay, bacteria, and scavengers did their damage.[64]

Regarding the objection relating to uniformitarianism, young-earth creationists reply that that the overwhelming force of a universal flood, combined with the rapid extermination of innumerable plants and animals, "could not fail to have been the greatest producer of thick sediments and entrapped plants and animals in those sediments of any event in world history."[65] They thus reject uniformitarianism and believe that the geological column is a record of what transpired in the flood.

In keeping with this, Dr. Bert Thompson, a Ph.D. in microbiology and former chairman of veterinary medicine at Texas A&M University, points out that in 1980 Mount St. Helen erupted and formed a 25-foot canyon in a mere 24 hours. Sediment layers were also laid down in extremely rapid fashion. Thompson thus urges that geological erosion can happen a lot faster than most uniformitarian proponents will admit.[66]

I discuss further differences of opinion between old-earthers and young-earthers in subsequent chapters.

4

The Fossils Argue Against Evolution

One of the more fascinating aspects of the study of origins has to do with the fossil evidence. This fascination is reflected in the popular media. Fossil discoveries are regularly reported in newspapers and magazines around the world. Television shows on the Discovery Channel and PBS feature the latest and greatest fossil discoveries. Movies like *Jurassic Park* and *The Lost World* feature fossils, dinosaur bones, dino-DNA, and more.

One of the best ways to become an instant celebrity is to discover fossils that "prove" evolution. Make a significant discovery, and you might just find yourself featured in the pages of *National Geographic* magazine.

On the darker side of fossil studies, research funding for continued fossil hunting is often dependent on a researcher's significant evolution-supporting discoveries. One cannot help but wonder whether such researchers are always completely objective regarding their interpretations of their findings.[1] The sad reality is that just as university professors must "publish or perish" in order to rise in the academic field, so paleontologists must find evolution-supporting fossils if they hope to rise in their field.

What Are Fossils?

Fossils point us to the past. They constitute rock-solid evidence of various life-forms, some of which have continued to exist to the present day and others that have become extinct. *Webster's Revised Unabridged Dictionary* defines a fossil as "the remains of an animal or plant found in stratified rocks."[2] Princeton University's WordNet database defines a fossil as "a relic or impression of a plant or animal that existed in a past geological age."[3] *The American Heritage Dictionary of the English Language* defines a fossil as "a remnant or trace of an organism of a past geologic age, such as a skeleton or leaf imprint, embedded and preserved in the earth's crust."[4] Actually, the word "fossil" comes from the Latin word *fossilis*, which literally means "dug up." Fossils, then, represent the mineralized remains, traces, and impressions of plants and animals that lived long ago and have since been dug up.[5] They are deposited and preserved for us in the layers (or "strata") of sedimentary rock that form the earth's crust.

Billions of fossils have been discovered virtually all over the world. Henry Morris notes that multiple fossils of fish have been discovered in such diverse areas as California, New York, and Scotland. Dinosaur graveyards are scattered all around, including such places as the Rockies, South Africa, Central Asia, and Belgium. Fossils of marine invertebrates are found almost everywhere.[6] Fossils of ocean fish, mollusk shells, and even a whale have been discovered on various mountains.[7]

Having noted this abundance of fossils, allow me to suggest a logical expectation: If evolutionary theory were true, one would expect that the fossil record would show a step-by-step progression from simple life-forms to increasingly complex life-forms. The record should show a step-by-step progression from common ancestors to the complex organisms of today. As we will see in this chapter, however, the fossil record actually shows that species throughout geologic history have remained remarkably stable (not changing) for exceedingly long periods of time, and that a sudden explosion of life-forms erupted during the Cambrian age (the first period of the Paleozoic era). Creationists therefore believe that the fossil evidence is much more in keeping with their view than with evolutionary theory.[8] No intermediate fossils showing a transition of one species into another have been found.

Darwin Had an Excuse

During Charles Darwin's day (the 1860s), only a portion of the fossil record in the various layers of the earth's crust had been uncovered and studied—though some discoveries of fossils in the Cambrian strata had been made. As scholar Michael Denton said in his book *Evolution: A Theory in Crisis,*

> In Darwin's day only a tiny fraction of all fossil bearing strata had been examined and the number of professional paleontologists could practically be counted on two hands. Huge areas of the globe had never been explored and certainly not examined by geologists and paleontologists. Large areas of the Soviet Union, Australia, Africa and most of Asia were practically untouched.[9]

Based on the limited discoveries of his time, a troubled Darwin wondered where all the fossil evidence was for his theory:

> Why then is not every geological formation and every stratum full of such intermediate links? Geology assuredly does not reveal any such finely-graduated organic chain; and this, perhaps, is the most obvious and serious objection which can be urged against the theory. The explanation lies, as I believe, in the extreme imperfection of the geological record.[10]

Some of the scientists living in Darwin's day criticized his theory for lack of evidence, but Darwin was able to temporarily disarm such criticism with his suggestion that the fossil record was incomplete. His hope was that further paleontological studies would unveil intermediates in the fossil record, thereby proving the evolution of one species into another. But even if such evidence failed to surface, Darwin suggested that it might be lacking only because the fossils in the earlier strata in the earth's crust might have been destroyed by heat and pressure.[11]

Since Darwin's day, evolutionists have continued to argue that the fossil record is imperfect. The late evolutionist Stephen Jay Gould said "we must work with the strictly limited evidence of a very imperfect fossil record."[12] Evolutionist Richard Dawkins uses an analogy of a film to make his point: "It is as though we had a cine film with most of the frames missing. We can, to be sure, see movement of a kind when we project our film of fossils, but it is more jerky than Charlie Chaplin, for even the oldest and scratchiest Charlie Chaplin film hasn't completely lost nine-tenths of its frames."[13]

Today, however, over a century after Darwin's time, an abundance of fossils have been discovered—virtually billions of them—more than enough to draw valid scientific conclusions, and they show rather conclusively that no intermediate fossils exist.[14] Further, as for the claim that fossils in the earlier strata in the earth's crust might have been destroyed by heat and pressure, fossil discoveries in the pre-Cambrian strata debunk this idea. Indeed, fossil discoveries in this strata reveal single-celled organisms that have *not* been destroyed—and if fossils of such small organisms were not destroyed, one cannot reasonably argue that fossils of larger organisms would have been destroyed.

The Cambrian Explosion

The fossil record shows no evidence of simple life-forms transitioning into complex life-forms. Rather, the evidence reveals a virtual explosion of animal phyla (divisions or "types" of the animal kingdom) appearing during the Cambrian era[15] with no true evolutionary ancestors in the Precambrian era and no truly new groups appearing in post-Cambrian times. Moreover, researchers have uncovered fossils of more than a hundred species of soft-bodied animals, innumerable small shelled organisms, and other life-forms.[16] So astonishing is the explosion of life-forms during the Cambrian period that some refer to it as "biology's big bang." Stephen Jay Gould explains it this way: "In one of the most crucial and enigmatic episodes in the history of life—and a challenge to the old and congenial idea that life has progressed in a basically stately and linear manner through the ages—nearly all animal phyla make their first appearance in the fossil record at essentially the same time."[17] Many of the animal types that appear in the Cambrian era continue to the present day.[18]

Some evolutionists, like Richard Dawkins, admit that these fossils of life-forms seemingly "were just planted there, without any evolutionary history behind them."[19] Honest evolutionists admit that this is a strike against Darwin's theory.[20] Other evolutionists seem not bothered, suggesting (without evidence) that the Cambrian explosion simply points to a very large (Precambrian) gap in the fossil record.[21]

An objective consideration of the Cambrian explosion reveals *no evolutionary descent* of life-forms and *no slow modifications* taking place in life-forms as a result of natural selection. Phillip Johnson is right in saying that "the prevailing characteristic of fossil species is *stasis*—the absence of change. There are numerous 'living fossils' which are much the same today as they were millions of years ago, at least as far as we can determine."[22]

Some evolutionists have tried to argue that the reason no fossil precursors exist prior to Cambrian times is that they were soft-bodied creatures and wouldn't have had any hard parts to be fossilized. Ernst Mayr, for example, writes that "the absence of the ancestral types in Precambrian strata can be explained if one assumes that the earliest multicellular animals were microscopically small and soft-bodied."[23] He argues that fossils showed up in the Cambrian strata because the organisms developed skeletons.[24] Steve Jones, professor of genetics at University College London, likewise writes that "the Cambrian Explosion, so called, is a failure of the geological record rather than of the Darwinian machine. Its radical new groups reflect not a set of exceptional events, but something more banal: the first appearance of animals with parts capable of preservation. Before then, there were soft creatures that decayed as soon as they died."[25] However, as noted previously, single-celled organisms have been discovered in the Precambrian strata, and *more than a hundred* species of soft-bodied animals have been uncovered in the Cambrian (and later) strata.[26] This evidence shows that soft-bodied creatures could have fossilized during Precambrian times.[27]

What does all this mean? It means that whether you are an old-earth creationist who interprets this Cambrian explosion as occurring between 525 and 550 million years ago[28] or a young-earth creationist who interprets the explosion as occurring less than 10,000 years ago, the end result is that the Cambrian evidence deals evolution a severe blow. The reason that life-forms appear to have been "just planted there" in the Cambrian era is that *they were* planted there—by a divine Creator.

Evolution's Big Problem: No Intermediate Fossils

The more one studies the fossil records, the more one finds a lack of evidence to support evolution. If evolution were true, one would expect to see in the fossil records progressively complex evolutionary forms, indicating transitions of one life-form into another. We should see fish transitioning into reptiles and some ancient ancestor life-form transitioning into apes and humans. However, out of all the billions of fossils known and documented in the rocks of the earth's crust, *no such evidence exists.*[29] The British Museum of History alone contains some 60 million fossil specimens, yet not one is a transitional form showing one species evolving into another.[30]

Rather, the evidence reveals a sudden appearance of life-forms, and each of them exhibits *all* the features that distinguish that life-form—*fully formed* and *fully functional*—with no evolving of body parts involved. We find no ancestors with stubs on their lower bodies that gave rise to species with legs. We find no ancestors with stubs on their sides that gave rise to species with wings. Such Darwinian "gradualism" is completely absent.

Stephen Jay Gould is an example of an evolutionist who has conceded that the lack of transitional evidence in the fossil record has been a problem for traditional evolutionism. He once commented that "all paleontologists know that the fossil record contains precious little in the way of intermediate forms; transitions between major groups are characteristically abrupt."[31] He said "the extreme rarity of transitional forms in the fossil record persists as the trade secret of paleontology."[32] He admitted that "the absence of fossil evidence for intermediary stages between major transitions in organic design, indeed our inability, even in our imagination, to construct functional intermediates in many cases, has been a persistent and nagging problem for gradualistic accounts of evolution."[33]

Darwin had earnestly hoped for countless examples in the fossil record showing transitions of one species into another. He asked, "Why, if species have descended from other species by insensibly fine graduations, do we not everywhere see innumerable transitional forms?"[34] To date, however, researchers have not discovered one true transitional form.

Evolutionist Claims of Transitional Discoveries

Some evolutionists have claimed that a transitional form in the fossil record is the archaeopteryx, which one will find illustrated in many textbooks used in public schools.[35] The archaeopteryx, discovered not long after Darwin published *On the Origin of Species,* is an extinct primitive bird that allegedly existed during the Jurassic period and had lizard-like characteristics such as teeth, claws on its wings, and a long bony tail, but also had feathers.[36] Evolutionists conclude that the archaeopteryx is a transitional form between reptiles and birds.

Creationists believe evolutionists are making too much of the archaeopteryx. One reason the archaeopteryx is not a true transitional form is that all of its body parts are fully formed and fully functional. Its wings are fully formed (perfectly suited to flight), its tail is fully formed (it is not a mere stub), its claws are fully formed (no sharp stubs), and nothing on the creature indicates it is in the process of developing from one species into another. It is simply a unique creature, perfectly compatible with a creationist scenario. In other words, the archaeopteryx had all these unique features because God created it that way.

Further, the evidence indicates that birds have been around as long as or before the archaeopteryx, so the archaeopteryx couldn't have been the ancient ancestor of birds that evolutionists hope for.[37] Indeed, researcher John Noble Wilford, based on a discovery in northeastern China, concluded that "by the time of archaeopteryx, another bird lineage with perhaps much more ancient origins existed. That lineage seems to have led to modern birds." Wilford says this new evidence of a sparrow-size bird called the liaoningornis—a virtual contemporary of the archaeopteryx—"casts serious doubt on the widely held theory that birds are direct descendants of dinosaurs."[38]

Did Evolution Have "Spurts"?

The fossil evidence argues against the evolutionary idea of gradualism—the idea that over long periods of time, species evolved into other species as a result of natural selection. In view of this, evolutionists Niles Eldredge and Stephen Jay Gould in 1972 proposed a theory known as "punctuated equilibrium."[39]

This theory suggests that the fossil record may not be as imperfect as everyone thought. "Maybe the 'gaps' are a true reflection of what really happened, rather than being the annoying but inevitable consequences of an imperfect fossil record."[40] According to this theory, the development of new species occurred in spurts of major genetic alterations that punctuate long periods of little change.[41] "The long period of stasis is the portion of the process referred to as the period of *equilibrium*, and the interval characterized by rapid evolution is a *punctuation*—thus the term, punctuated equilibrium."[42]

More precisely, this theory postulates that evolution is sometimes in stasis and no evolution occurs. When evolution does occur, it happens in rapid spurts of major genetic alterations where new species can arise. These rapid spurts punctuate (periodically interrupt) long periods of time. These spurts of evolution are typically followed by a long period of stasis.

According to this view, rapid spurts of evolution take place as a result of specific creatures being geographically cut off from other members of their species. In their struggle to survive in a new inhospitable area (an area in which great "selective pressure" is put upon them to change so they can adapt to their more difficult environment), the creatures quickly evolve (that is, over tens of thousands of years), and their favorable variations are then passed on to offspring.[43] These newly evolved creatures eventually move back into more mainstream geological areas where they die and become fossilized. This appears in the fossil record as an abrupt change in species with new fully-formed features.[44] This new species then dies off by extinction or proliferates into a large population.

An obvious problem for the theory of punctuated equilibrium is that it calls loud attention to the utter lack of transitional forms in the fossil record. It is like a giant neon sign pointing to the fact that stasis (no change) is what we witness in the fossil record. One strongly suspects that since no transitional forms have been found in the fossil record, this theory was formulated to explain away the lack of evidence. Virtually no empirical biological evidence for the theory exists. The evidence simply reveals an explosion of animal phyla during the Cambrian era.

A second major problem with punctuated equilibrium is that it goes against all that is known regarding mutations. Studies in DNA and genetics indicate that a particular species has sufficient genetic potential to give rise to all kinds of variety *within* that species but not to transform it into an entirely new species.[45] So, for example, variations have occurred within the "dog kind," but we never witness the dog evolving into another species. Variations have occurred within the "cat kind," but we never witness the cat evolving into another species. Should a dog be isolated off from other dogs in an inhospitable area, it may change in the *micro*evolutionary sense (changes within the dog species) but not in the *macro*evolutionary sense (with dogs evolving into another species). Later in the book I discuss how typical mutations do not add information to the DNA but rather remove information, making the organism weaker in some way.

The Fantasy World of Darwinism

All things considered, the fossil evidence is truly discouraging for Darwinists. An objective look at the fossils shows not only a lack of evidence *for* evolution, but provides extensive evidence *against* evolution. Understandably, Dr. Michael Denton concludes:

> Not only has paleontology failed spectacularly to come up with the fossil "missing links" which Darwin anticipated, but hypothetical reconstructions of major evolutionary developments—such as that linking birds to reptiles—are beginning to look more like fantasies than serious conjectures.[46]

"Ape-Men" Discoveries Do Not Prove Evolution

When I was a young boy, I remember seeing an evolution program on television that portrayed our alleged ancestors—the so-called "ape-men." They walked upright, were hairy all over (though not quite as hairy as an ape), had large, flat foreheads with pronounced brows, and seemed savage. Not knowing any better at the time, I remember asking my older brother Paul if all this was true. He assured me it was. (Of course, he was also very young at the time and had no idea what he was talking about.)

The images I saw on television that day stuck with me. I think the sudden and disturbing realization that I had descended from these ape-men caused the images to be permanently imprinted on my brain. In any event, only years later—after I became a Christian at age 17—did I revisit the issue and determine that I had believed a fiction.

I discovered that every once in a while, skulls and bones had been discovered in different parts of the world that caused unbridled excitement among paleontologists. The reason so much excitement accompanied these discoveries was that they were believed to represent ancient ancestors of modern humans and therefore constitute ironclad proof for evolutionary theory. These discoveries were assigned names, the most famous being Neanderthal man, Java man, Piltdown man, Peking man, Nebraska man, and East Africa ape.

Evolutionists believe that humans and apes evolved from a common ancestor.[1] The split or divergence from this common ancestor (a species "fork in the road," as it were) is said to have occurred between five and eight million years ago (scholars debate this issue).[2] According to this theory, after the "split" occurred, one evolutionary line eventually (after many stages of development) culminated in true man between one and three million years ago. In proof of this, evolutionists offer evidence of fossil *hominoids* (which includes apes and humans) and *homonids* (primates in the line allegedly leading to modern humans but still subhuman in nature).[3]

Ernst Mayr is representative of many evolutionists when he asserts that "no well-informed person any longer questions the descent of man from primates and more specifically from apes. The evidence for this conclusion is simply too overwhelming."[4] In support of this statement, Mayr cites the similar anatomy of humans and apes as well as the similarity of the DNA between the two.[5]

In what follows, I take a brief look at some of the more important "ape-men" discoveries of recent times and also briefly address the anatomy and DNA similarities between humans and apes.

Neanderthal Man

Johann C. Fuhlrott found Neanderthal man in 1856 in Neander Valley, near Dusseldorf, Germany. He discovered a skull and several bones. The skull, we are told, is characterized by a flat, retreating forehead, allegedly denoting limited intellect. At the time, Neanderthal man was thought to be an early "ape-man"—a savage, brutish, semierect subhuman. Researchers claimed that his spine lacked the curves to allow him to walk fully erect.[6] He walked on the edge of his feet, unlike modern humans. He seemed a natural transition between apes and humans, being viewed as part ape and part human.[7]

Beginning in the 1950s however, scholars began to change their minds, especially in view of the fact that similar remains have been discovered in Europe, Africa, and Asia.[8] The evidence now suggests that these were the bones of a hunched-over man who suffered severely from rickets, a disease caused by a severe vitamin D deficiency.[9] This condition causes a softening of the bones as well as defective bone growth. Those who have this disease are characterized by a bulky head, a crooked spine and limbs, and depressed ribs, among other things.

Today Neanderthal man has been recategorized as truly human and, creationists believe, is a descendant of Noah.[10] He was very muscular, powerful, and thickset,[11] but such features are certainly within the gene pool for humanity. Such robusticity can be found on an individual basis in modern living populations today.[12] Some scholars suggest that the reason for his muscular, stocky body relates to the tough environment in which he lived. His robusticity was due to the hard labor he had to engage in just to survive.[13]

The evidence shows that Neanderthal man, when in good health, stood fully erect and walked in a normal fashion with a normal posture like modern humans.[14] He certainly had a fully human brain capacity.[15] The evidence shows that he sewed clothes from animal skins, built shelters, had a form of writing, practiced religious ceremonies, played musical instruments, made and used various tools (including axes, borers, scrapers, points, and knives[16]), fashioned stone arrowheads, used fire for cooking, painted pictures, used language to communicate, buried the dead, and even placed flowers upon graves. Sometimes he buried the dead with various objects, suggesting the possibility that he had some kind of belief in the afterlife.[17] He also displayed social care. "Some skeletons show the marks of obvious injuries or illnesses suffered sometime before death, evidence that there must have been social care to support certain ailing or disabled individuals."[18] These are not things one would expect of a savage apelike creature.[19] Clearly, Neanderthal man was a Homo sapiens.[20]

Java Man *(Pithecanthropus Erectus)*

Java man, also known as *Pithecanthropus erectus* (Greek: *pithecos* = ape, *anthropos* = man, *erectus* = erect, and thus "erect ape-man"[21]), was discovered by a Dutch physician named Eugene Dubois in Trinil, Java in 1891. Dubois had no formal geological or paleontological training, and his search team consisted of prison convicts under the surveillance of a couple of army corporals.[22]

Dubois discovered a single skull cap and a tooth about a month apart. At first, he thought these items belonged to a chimpanzee (the cranial capacity was certainly much smaller than that of a human[23]). Later, however, a thigh bone (femur) that obviously belonged to a human appeared, and Dubois revised his thinking about the skull cap and tooth, concluding that all these items belonged to one animal named *Pithecanthropus erectus*.[24] He dated this find at about 500,000 years old.

Dubois's discovery was met with mixed reaction. Some experts, such as Rudolph Virchow (who founded the science of pathology), doubted that these items belonged to a single individual. He said, "In my opinion, this creature was an animal, a giant gibbon, in fact. The thigh bone has not the slightest connection with the skull."[25] Other experts felt that all the items were essentially apelike. Still others considered them to be human. Today, most experts in the field consider the *Pithecanthropus erectus* to be an extinct, giant gibbon-like creature (an arboreal ape) that bears no relation to humans.[26] This creature is not the transitional link evolutionists were hoping for.

Piltdown Man (*Eanthropus Dawsoni*)

Charles Dawson discovered Piltdown man, also known as *Eanthropus dawsoni* ("dawn man"), in 1912 in Piltdown, England. The discovery included a dark brown skull, a jawbone, and a few teeth, and was said to be the remains of an ape-man who lived at least 500,000 years ago (perhaps even 750,000 years ago). Such esteemed scholars as Dr. Arthur Smith Woodward, paleontologist at the British Museum, and Dr. Henry Fairfield Osborn, paleontologist of the American Museum of Natural History, were fully convinced of the validity and significance of this ape-man discovery.[27] Osborn believed the discovery proved man had descended from apes in view of its apelike and humanlike anatomical characteristics.[28]

Unfortunately for evolutionists, and to the great embarrassment of scholars like Woodward and Osborn, Piltdown man turned out to be a hoax![29] Close examination in 1953 revealed that the skull looked relatively normal for a human, but the jaw looked primitive and apelike.[30] This led some scholars to doubt the association between the two. Tests then revealed that the jawbone was that of a female orangutan, and it had been intentionally stained in order to make it appear to match the dark brown human skull.[31] Further, the teeth on the lower (orangutan) jaw had quite obviously been filed down to match the teeth on the upper jaw (the file marks were visible).[32] Still further, researcher Rod Caird notes that the skull and lower jaw had been "placed at the appropriate level in the gravel pit alongside imported mammal fossils from the correct period in order to substantiate the dating." Hence, Caird concludes, this was "an absolutely deliberate and careful fraud."[33]

What is highly disturbing is that Piltdown man was first discovered in 1912, but was not exposed as a fraud until 1953—*over four decades later.* Some observers are understandably baffled at the apparent ineptness of the scientists involved. The issue of concern: *What took you so long?* The perpetrator of this fraud has not been firmly established.[34]

The Piltdown man fraud is not the only such fraud to deceive scientists (and the public). Researcher James Perloff warns:

> Those who think such mistakes no longer occur need only consider the archaeoraptor, promoted in a 10-page color spread in the November 1999 *National Geographic* as the "true missing link" between dinosaurs and birds. The fossil was displayed at National Geographic's Explorers Hall and viewed by over 100,000 people. However, it too turned out to be a fake—someone had simply glued together fragments of bird and dinosaur fossils.[35]

Peking Man

Davidson Bolack discovered Peking man in 1912 near Peking, China. The discovery consisted of over a hundred teeth, thirty skulls, and some tools. Again, many people hoped that this would be a significant ape-man discovery. Mysteriously, however, by the end of World War II all the skulls disappeared. Meanwhile, Bolack died of a heart attack.

Many scholars who have studied the discovery have now concluded that the skulls and teeth represent the remains of monkeys or baboons that had been killed and eaten by lime quarry workers.[36] The tools discovered alongside the skulls and teeth were apparently used by the workers to extract the brains of these monkeys so they could be eaten. (Monkey brains were considered a delicacy.)[37] In any event, Peking man is certainly not a transitional ape-man.

Nebraska Man

Geologist Harold Cook discovered Nebraska man in western Nebraska in 1922. Actually, Cook only discovered a single solitary tooth. *Just a tooth!* Yet paleontologists claimed this discovery was a link in man's evolution. A London newspaper hired an artist to draw a picture of the one-million-year-old ape-man that belonged to the tooth. The artist also drew "Nebraska mom."[38] The male ape-man was portrayed holding a club, while the ape-woman was portrayed gathering roots. This tooth-to-drawing extrapolation truly smacks of desperation.

Unfortunately for evolutionists, this discovery did not turn out to be the evidence they were hoping for. Harold Cook discovered another identical tooth—this time attached to a skull and skeleton. But it wasn't the skull and skeleton of an ape-man but rather an extinct wild pig.[39] So much for Nebraska man.

Related to this, I must confess that a spark of indignation rises in my heart when I read about the Scopes Evolution Trial in Dayton, Tennessee in July 1925. In this trial, a defender of the Bible named William Jennings Bryan was ridiculed and berated for his lack of knowledge regarding this amazing discovery of Nebraska man. And all the while—though yet unknown to all present—it was just a pig's tooth!

East African Ape *(Zinjanthropus)*

Louis S.B. Leakey discovered East African ape, also known as *Zinjanthropus*, in 1959 in Olduvia, Tanzania. The discovery consisted of a skull cap and some fragments of bone. This ape-man link, dated at two to four million years old, was featured in *National Geographic Magazine* as a support for evolution.

Again, however, the supposed significance of the discovery turned out to be nothing. In 1965, professor Phillip Tobias of the University of the Witwatersrand thoroughly examined and measured the skull and found that it belonged to a variety of Southern ape *(Australopithecus)*.[40]

Lucy

Donald Johanson discovered Lucy in Ethiopia in 1974. The discovery consisted of the skeletal remains—about 40 percent intact[41]—of a female hominid and was categorized as

Australopithecus afarensis and dated at three million years old. Lucy could supposedly walk upright like a human.

Scholars have made special note of Lucy's small apelike brain-case, comparable in size to those of chimpanzees when measured relative to overall body size (the brain was estimated to be about one-fourth the size of that of a human[42]). The jaws and face were apelike.[43] Lucy's teeth were far larger than those of a human. She was probably about three feet, six inches tall and weighed less than 60 pounds, far less than a human.[44] Scholars have also noted that the hands and feet of other more recent *Australopithecus afarensis* discoveries are chimpanzee-like and not human. Indeed, the hands and feet are typically long and curved, common among tree-dwelling apes that swing on branches.[45] As for the claim that Lucy could walk upright, the evidence reveals she could walk *somewhat* upright, much like pygmy chimps do today. She certainly could not walk *fully* upright like human beings. Lucy's knee structure points more to tree-climbing abilities than the ability to walk upright.[46]

Because of such evidence, Lucy has been dismissed as an ancestor for man—not just by creationists but by respected secularists. Britain's Lord Solly Zuckerman, an authority on the *Australopithecus*, concluded that the evidence that this animal walked upright is extremely flimsy. Charles Oxnard, former professor of anatomy at the University of Southern California Medical School, did a computer analysis of the *Australopithecus* skeleton and concluded that it is "now irrevocably removed" from a place in the evolution of man's ability to walk on two feet and "from any place in the direct human lineage."[47]

What Conclusions Can We Draw?

In this chapter we have seen that:

- Neanderthal man turned out to be not an ape-man but rather truly human.

- Java man turned out to be an arboreal ape.

- Piltdown man turned out to be a colossal hoax.

- Peking man turned out to be a monkey.

- Nebraska man turned out to be a wild pig.

- Lucy was apparently a chimpanzee.

Yet, in each case, when these discoveries were made, the popular media reported them as hard proof for evolution theory. Even evolutionists have observed how sensational the press reports can be. Richard Fortey writes:

> Every discovery of a new hominid fossil makes the news. The reports that have appeared in the newspapers over the years are interesting for the light they cast upon the psychology of both scientist and the reporter. I have never seen a new discovery reported as SMALL TOEBONE ADDS DETAIL TO AFRICAN HOMINID. It is always something like NEW FIND OF FOSSIL MAN OVERTURNS GENESIS, and the accounts nearly always include phrases claiming that the textbooks will now have to be rewritten.[48]

Despite all the media hoopla about alleged ape-men, however, *no hard evidence yet exists for their reality*. To be sure, we do have lots of fossils and bones of human beings, and we do have lots of fossils and bones of apes, but we do not have any fossils or bones of transitional ape-men, nor do we have any fossils demonstrating that human beings and apes derived from a common ancestor. The fossil record seems to indicate that apes have always been apes and humans have always been humans.[49] Though evolutionists do not want to hear it, this is perfectly compatible with what the Bible teaches regarding creationism.[50]

Richard Milton, author of the book *Shattering the Myths of Darwinism*, reveals a pattern in all these ape-men discoveries.

> The pattern is a recurring one. The remains themselves are always meager. The first attribution is always that the being whose remains have been discovered shows both human and ape characteristics, and is therefore a genuine transitional type—a real missing link. Then the attribution is questioned: the characters ascribed to apes are actually within the range of human characters;… or the reconstruction work is over imaginative; sometimes simple mistakes of identification are made perhaps due to disease or malformation of bones.[51]

Milton goes on to point out that in each case, what researchers thought was a transitional link is either an ape or a human. And such reassignments have been accepted by all but evolutionary fanatics.[52]

Even some evolutionists have expressed doubt about alleged discoveries of man's ancestors. In his book *Darwin's Ghost: The Origin of Species Updated*, Steve Jones writes:

> In spite of a century's claims of the discovery of "missing links," it is quite possible that no bone yet found is on the direct genetic line to ourselves. With so many kinds to choose from, so few remains of each, and such havoc among the relics, none of the fossils may have direct descendants today.[53]

We can easily understand why *Time* magazine reported:

> Despite more than a century of digging, the fossil record remains maddeningly sparse. With so few clues,

> even a single bone that doesn't fit into the picture
> can upset everything. Virtually every major discovery
> has put deep cracks in the conventional wisdom and
> forced scientists to concoct new theories, amid furi-
> ous debate.[54]

To throw one more wrench into the evolutionary hypothesis, people today have all kinds of different shapes. Just walk
down a crowded street in a busy city and you will see what I
mean. Skull shapes alone show all kinds of variety among
modern humans. When we evaluate evidence from the past,
looking at various skull discoveries, we can easily make false and
subjective assumptions regarding how *this* skull or *that* skull must
have been ancient ancestors to modern humans because of the
way they are shaped. Researchers would do well to keep in mind
the wide diversity of skull shapes among extant human beings.

What about evolutionist Ernst Mayr's argument that
human evolution is proved because of the similar anatomy
between humans and apes? Creationists have never disputed that
many animals in the world have obviously similar body appearances, including human beings and apes. However, this does not
demand that one descended from the other, or that they have
a common ancestor. That the Creator would design many of
His creatures with obvious similarities—such as eyes, ears, noses,
mouths, arms, legs, and so forth (with similar DNA)—makes
perfectly good sense because such characteristics are best suited
for living in the similar environment in which God has placed
us all. God in His wisdom knows that certain designs work best.

I close with the observation that while evolutionists often
accuse creationists of being unscientific, the evidence in this chapter suggests that evolutionists have repeatedly tried to pass off
science fiction as true science. In view of this, we should not be
disturbed the next time we read in the newspaper of some discovery presenting ironclad "proof" for the theory of evolution.

Mutations and Natural Selection Cannot Bring About New Species

Evolution cannot occur without innumerable positive mutations occurring over an extremely long time. Darwinists believe that such positive mutations are preserved by natural selection to bring about not only changes *within* species but also *entirely new* species. As theologian Charles Ryrie put it, "mutations + natural selection + time = evolution."[1]

A mutation may be defined as "a change of the DNA sequence within a gene or chromosome of an organism resulting in the creation of a new character or trait not found in the parental type."[2] In other words, since DNA contains genetic information, a mutation involves some kind of change in that information so that a new character or trait emerges in the organism.

How do such mutations occur? Several possible causes exist. Small random copying errors of the commands of the DNA's genetic code often occur.[3] One expert notes that "each living cell has an intricate molecular machinery designed for the copying of DNA, the genetic molecule. But as in other copying processes mistakes do occur, although not very often. Once in every 10,000–100,000 copies a gene will contain a mistake."[4] These kinds of copying errors do not happen very often because "the cell has machinery for correcting these mistakes."[5] Other causes of mutations are external, such as being exposed to radiation (like X-rays), mustard gas, or highly toxic chemicals.[6]

Michael Behe illustrates a mutation (a change in DNA) with an analogy. If you compare DNA to a step-by-step list of instructions—for example, to build a motorcycle—a mutation might be likened to a change in one of the lines of instructions. For example, instead of "Attach the seat to the top of the engine," the instructions might be changed to read, "Attach the seat to the handlebars."[7] This "mutation" would obviously be deleterious to the motorcycle. Similarly, a change in the information in human DNA (due to a negative mutation) might be deleterious and cause a human to be born without a limb.

In evolutionary theory, mutations are directly related to natural selection, a concept I introduced in chapter 1. Natural selection involves the idea that each species typically produces far more members than can possibly be supported by the environment. In view of this, a struggle for survival entails with each member vying for the limited resources in the environment. This struggle has winners and losers. The winners are typically the more superior of the species, and the losers are typically the more inferior. The winners survive and pass on their superior characteristics to their offspring, and the losers die off.[8]

The winners also allegedly develop ever-new characteristics that enhance the possibility of survival.[9] An organism—typically due to harsh environmental demands—may pass on positive mutational changes to offspring, causing them to develop positive characteristics the parents did not have, characteristics that give a competitive advantage for survival and enhance fitness.[10] (A polar bear in a cold environment might pass on a positive mutation to its offspring, causing a thicker coat of hair.) These offspring with positive new characteristics are then preserved by natural selection.[11] An organism that develops a negative characteristic due to a negative mutation does not survive, and that negative characteristic is bred out of the evolutionary line of development. This process is described as "survival of the fittest."[12]

This process is believed to repeat itself generation by generation. Over a very long period of time, many such positive mutational changes occur, the result being that the organism grows increasingly complex and may evolve into an entirely different species with novel features.[13] Evolutionists suggest that such positive mutations account for how all life developed on earth from a single-celled living organism (an organism which itself somehow naturally emerged from nonlife). Of course, the long transition from a single-celled organism to a complex life-form like a human being would demand literally trillions upon trillions of positive mutational changes.

What if a particular organism was already well adapted and well suited to its particular environment? Darwinian theory holds that in such a case, if the environment remains stable and no subsequent mutations occur, then no evolutionary development will take place in that organism. In such a case there is no environmental pressure for mutational changes to take place.[14] (Natural selection apparently holds to the idea, "If it's not broke, don't fix it.") This may account for the fact, evolutionists say, that some species seem not to change over long periods of time.

Does Natural Selection Ever Occur?

One purpose of this book is to argue against the possibility of Darwinian evolution, which places great stock in natural selection. But in arguing against the idea that natural selection can cause one species to transition into another, one might surmise that natural selection never occurs at all. This would be a wrong conclusion.

The evidence is clear that natural selection does occur in our world, but it always involves limited changes *within* species. A popular textbook example of natural selection involves peppered moths resting upon tree trunks.[15] Such moths can be either black or white. According to evolutionary lore, a situation arose in a village in England in which the tree trunks became covered with a light-colored fungus. At this time, allegedly 98 percent of the peppered moths were white. The black moths did not survive because they were easy prey for birds (with their dark bodies against the light background of the fungus). The white-colored moths were more safe, for they were camouflaged as they rested upon the lightly colored fungus on the tree trunks. However, pollution soon increased in the area and killed the fungus on the tree trunks. Now, because the dark bark on the tree trunks became visible, the white moths became easy prey for birds (with their light bodies against the dark background). The percentage allegedly shifted to 98 percent black moths.[16]

The problem with this account is that Jonathan Wells, in an article entitled "Second Thoughts on Peppered Moths" (*The Scientist*, May 1999), provided convincing proof that moths typically do not ever land on tree trunks during the day. He noted that during 25 years of research with peppered moths, the moths had been seen to land on tree trunks only twice. Most of the time they land on higher branches in the tree. This undermines the whole peppered moth "proof" for natural selection.[17] But even if the account were legitimate, it would simply be a demonstration of natural selection *within* a species. Certainly the account tells us nothing about how the moth originally came into being and gives no hint of the moth evolving into another species.[18] As creationist John Morris puts it, "Variation within a specific created type occurs all the time. Natural selection can select the variant best suited for an environment, but natural selection does not create anything new."[19]

Another example of in-species natural selection involves some small birds called finches in the Galapagos Islands. Apparently, as a result of a drought in 1977, the finches found themselves without the small seeds they were accustomed to eating. They had no choice but to eat larger seeds. Some of the smaller finches, however, ended up dying because the seeds were too big for them. Within a generation, the size of the finches—their beaks included—increased to accommodate the environmental situation.[20]

Though the peppered moth and finch examples are often cited by evolutionists as proofs of general evolutionary theory, the reality is that they only prove microevolution. Earlier in the book I noted that microevolution refers to changes that occur within the same species, while macroevolution refers to the transition or evolution of one species into another. In the above examples (assuming the peppered moth story is legitimate, for the sake of argumentation), notice that the peppered moth always remained a peppered moth. While the peppered moth may have experienced changes within the species (going from a light color to a dark color), the peppered moth never evolved into another species. Likewise, notice that the finch always remained a finch. While the finch did experience changes within the species (growing larger), the finch never evolved into another species.[21] Hence, we can see that while natural selection does occur *within* species, never does one species evolve into another. Mutations involve changes in existing organisms; they do not produce new ones.[22]

Richard Milton points out that genetic mutations can account for minor changes like blue eyes rather than brown, or tall rather than short. But mutations can never account for the emergence of a characteristic not already contained in the gene pool of a species.[23] Yet what *is* contained in the gene pool is vast indeed. Creationist Lane Lester tells us that

> an essential feature of the creation model is the placement of considerable genetic variety in each created kind. Only thus can we explain the possible origin of horse, donkeys, and zebras from the same kind; of lions, tigers, and leopards from the same kind; of some 118

varieties of the domestic dog, as well as jackals, wolves, and foxes from the same kind. As each kind obeyed the Creator's command to be fruitful and multiply, the chance processes of recombination and the more purposeful process of natural selection caused each kind to subdivide into the vast array we now see.[24]

Creationist Gary Parker tells us that so much genetic variety is built into human DNA that

the average human couple could have 10^{2017} children before they would have to have one child identical to another! That number, a one followed by 2017 zeroes, is greater than the number of sand grains by the sea, the number of stars in the sky, or the atoms in the known universe (a "mere" 10^{80}).[25]

The point is that the gene pool of each species allows for plenty of variation within that species.

We might argue that this ability for a species to develop new and better characteristics is an indication of intelligent design. After all, even human engineers design machines with a certain built-in adaptability. For example, my computer system is plugged into a mechanism that maintains a steady, unwavering flow of electrical current into my computer. If the power surges for some reason, this mechanism adapts and dampens the amount of electricity that flows into my computer. If for some reason the electrical power dips or even goes entirely off, this mechanism adapts to the situation and has a built-in battery that automatically flows that steady level of power into my computer so it will not crash. This mechanism adapts to change in the (electrical) environment, as it were. If humans are capable of such design, should we not assume that God would build a certain amount of adaptation into each species that enables that species to adapt to its environment?

Of course, as noted above, such changes have limits, for the DNA in each member of the species will ensure that each member of the species will *remain* a member of that species and not develop into a *new* species. The "kinds" of Genesis 1 have never crossed over and can never cross over. G.J. Mendel's experiments in plant genetics proved that the range of variation possible within a species was narrowly limited to the genetic parameters of that species, and offered no possibility of development into a different species.[26]

How Does Natural Selection Know What to Do?

Creationists grant that limited changes can occur in each species due to natural selection, but the evolutionary view that natural selection can bring about incredibly complex changes over a long, long time is a different story. Even Charles Darwin understood the seriousness of this issue, for he himself pondered how natural selection could have possibly given rise to the eye.

> To suppose the eye with all its inimitable contrivances for adjusting the focus to different distances, for admitting different amounts of light, and for the correction of spherical and chromatic aberration, could have been formed by natural selection, seems, I freely confess, absurd in the highest degree.[27]

The problem is that mutations only bring about one small change at a time, and the development of a complex organ like an eye would require multiple positive mutations. How would natural selection, at each minimal step along the way, know whether to keep each small mutational change or breed that small mutational change out of the species? How would natural selection recognize the worth of a single mutation during a long process of multiple mutations, awaiting the eventual arrival of a complex organ like an eye? How would natural selection know that a small flap of skin on the side of the body would in many generations be a wing, and thus decide to keep that flap of skin?[28] Since at every step along the way, the individual small mutational changes have no obvious immediate benefit, why wouldn't natural selection breed that change out of the species? I do not believe evolutionists have any good answer for this problem.

One must keep in mind that natural selection, according to evolutionists, is not "intelligent." Rather it is said to be a mindless process. Evolutionist Richard Dawkins declared:

> Natural selection, the blind, unconscious, automatic process which Darwin discovered, and which we know is the explanation for the existence and apparently purposeful form of all life, has no purpose in mind. It has no mind and no mind's eye. It does not plan for the future. It has no vision, no foresight, no sight at all. If it can be said to play the role of watchmaker in nature, it is the blind watchmaker.[29]

Likewise, evolutionist Ernst Mayr writes that "selection is not teleological (goal-directed).... Selection does not have a long-term goal." He argues that "there is no known genetic mechanism that could produce goal-directed evolutionary processes."[30] Evolution has *no* intelligent deterministic element.

Because natural selection is a mindless, blind, unconscious, purposeless process, it is not capable of making and fulfilling long-range goals. And if it cannot make and fulfill long-range goals, how could natural selection bring about the development of an eye, step-by-step, generation by generation, over a long period of time? Such a concept stretches the limits of credulity.

To compound the problem, the eye is only one among many complex organs in a human being. What about the ear? What about the brain? What about the heart? The liver? The kidney?

The nervous system? The nose, with its sense of smell? Are we to believe that again and again, natural selection blindly and mindlessly brought about complex organs via a step-by-step, generation-by-generation process over a long period of time? No wonder Darwin expressed doubts about how this could work. To imagine that natural selection could blindly and mindlessly construct a complex organ like an eye or ear makes about as much sense as imagining that dropping my television would result in an improved version.

The Harmfulness of Most Mutations

So far I have argued that evolutionism depends on virtually trillions of positive mutations in order for simple life-forms to evolve into complex life-forms. The big problem for this theory, however, is that most mutations—over 99 percent[31]—are harmful, destructive, and disadvantageous to the organism.[32] One textbook notes:

> Experiments have conclusively shown that most mutations are harmful (about 99.9%), and some are even deadly. Mutations seem to result from "accidents" which occur in the genes, and the chance that such an accident could be helpful rather than harmful is very small indeed. Two-headed snakes and albino squirrels are considered to be genetic disasters instead of the beginnings of new and more advanced creatures.[33]

Most mutations cause deterioration and breakdown in the organism. Such changes tend to make the organism less suited for its environment, thereby threatening its survival. One does not have to be a rocket scientist to know that if most mutations are destructive to an organism, then a series of *multiple* mutations will be much more likely to harm that organism. This fact greatly undermines evolutionary theory. As creationist Hugh Ross put it:

> While it is beyond dispute that life forms have changed very significantly over the course of the history of planet Earth, only micro-evolutionary changes have been determined to occur by strictly natural processes.... Natural selection can move a species only a limited distance from the species' norm, and the greater the distance, the lower the probability for survival.[34]

Evolutionists hope, however, that given enough time (millions of years), positive mutations might bring about new species. This is wishful thinking. More time will not change the outcome. Even in a million years, a television will *never* become a better television by dropping it on the floor. It will always remain the television that it is—except that it will probably break when it hits the floor.

If mutations were to bring about new species, they would have to add tremendous amounts of *new information* to the DNA (which carries genetic information). However, numerous studies and experiments have demonstrated that not only do mutations fail to produce new information, they actually delete information and harm the organism.[35] Mutations generally involve some kind of copying error in the DNA—genetic typos[36]—and are incapable of increasing information. This shows the absurdity of thinking that over a long period of time, enough information was added to cause a single-celled organism to eventually evolve into a complex human being with a brain, eyes, ears, a nose, a heart, kidneys, a liver, and all the other complex organs. For any of the above *individual* complex organs to develop through mutations is inconceivable, and the idea that these multiple complex organs evolved in a single species so as

to *function with each other as an interrelated whole* through positive mutations is beyond all comprehension. How could these
"parts" evolve in unison with the other parts?[37] We must remember that natural selection is mindless and blind. Macroevolution
would thus seem to be impossible.

Related to all this, as we examine the fossil record, we find
animals with fully developed eyes or wings, but we find *no intermediate animals* in the process of developing eyes or wings. We
find no animals, for example, with a small flap of skin on the
side that would in many generations evolve into a wing. This
is not what we'd expect to see if evolutionary theory were true.

What Can We Conclude?

In this chapter we have seen that

- Natural selection does occur in our world, but it always
  occurs within species. Never does natural selection cause
  one species to transform into another.

- The evidence supports limited variation within fixed
  boundaries (microevolution).

- Because natural selection is a mindless, blind, unconscious, purposeless process, it is not capable of making
  and fulfilling long-range goals. Natural selection cannot
  bring about the development of complex organs like the
  eye through a process that works mutation by mutation,
  step-by-step, generation by generation, over a long period
  of time.

- Over 99 percent of all mutations are harmful, destructive, and disadvantageous to the organism.

- The impossibility of positive mutations bringing about
  new species is rooted in the fact that this would require
  tremendous amounts of *new information* being added to

DNA (which carries genetic information). Typically, mutations *delete* information in the DNA.

In view of all this, we may conclude that the evidence argues strongly against evolution through positive mutations as guided by natural selection. William Dembski, in his book *Intelligent Design: The Bridge Between Science & Theology*, sums it up best by noting numerous problems for the mutation-selection mechanism of Darwinism, including (but not limited to) the emergence of life from nonlife, the origin of the genetic code in DNA (along with its vast information), the origin of multicellular life, the lack of intermediates in the fossil record, the explosion of life during the Cambrian period, and the development of what Dembski calls "irreducibly complex molecular machines."[38] Evolution is clearly fighting an uphill battle.

7

Comparative Anatomy, Vestigial Organs, and the Recapitulation Theory Do Not Prove Evolution

Evolutionists commonly argue in favor of their position by appealing to the marked similarities between the anatomy of man and that of the higher vertebrates, thereby "proving" that man evolved from an animal ancestor. This is the "comparative anatomy" argument.

Evolutionists also often argue that since human bodies contain some organs that have no known use, they must be "left-over" organs from an earlier animal stage. This is the "vestigial organ" argument.

Still further, some evolutionists have argued that as an embryo develops within the womb, it repeats *(recapitulates)* the evolutionary history of its species. Therefore, at various stages in embryonic development, it appears as a single-celled marine organism, a worm, a fish, an amphibian, a mammal, and finally a human. These stages involve the embryo displaying "vestigial remnants" of its past evolutionary history.[1] This is the "recapitulation" argument.

Let's take a brief look at these arguments to see if they have any validity.[2]

Answering Arguments from Comparative Anatomy

Evolutionists often argue for their theory by appealing to the marked similarities between the anatomy of man and that of the higher vertebrates, thereby "proving" that man evolved from an animal ancestor.[3] At first glance, this may seem a convincing argument for evolution. In reality, however, the theory is highly speculative and involves vast unwarranted assumptions based on naturalism (see chapter 2 for a debunking of this philosophy).

Creationists believe that similar organs among various animals are quite compatible with a creationist scenario. Human beings and all the animals were created by the same Creator, so we would expect some similarities in their design. When we observe the paintings of da Vinci, we note certain similarities between them, even though they portray different subjects. When we observe the paintings of Picasso, we note certain similarities between them, even though they portray different subjects. When we observe the paintings of even a modern painter like Thomas Kinkade, we note certain similarities between them, even though they portray different subjects. Likewise, when we observe the creations of the Creator (a divine Artist), we note certain similarities even though each species is different.[4]

Do not human engineers and designers do much the same thing in terms of incorporating similar design into various inventions? Wheels work well on cars, buses, tractors, wagons, bicycles, and tricycles. Light bulbs work well in houses, offices, cars, outdoor stadiums, and streetlamps. Air conditioners work fabulously in cars, houses, and other buildings. Glass lenses work wonderfully for eyeglasses, telescopes, and microscopes. If human designers can incorporate similar items into the things they make, surely the divine Creator could do the same with the creatures He made.

The environment is a key factor. Creationists believe that God in His wisdom, knowing that various species would be living and moving about in a similar environment, would endow these various creatures with body parts suitable to survival in that environment. For example, God would give them lungs since they would all be breathing the same air. God would give them stomachs and digestive tracts since they would be eating much of the same food. He would give them eyes so they could see where they were going, and ears to hear sounds in their environment, and noses to detect aromas. In each case, God designed an organ or body part that worked effectively, and He put this effective working part in various creatures. Similar anatomies make a strong case for a common Creator!

Answering Arguments from Vestigial Organs

Evolutionists have often argued that bodily organs with no known use must be "leftover" organs from an earlier animal stage at which time they were useful (for example, they may have been useful for Neanderthals or other cave-dwellers). Because such vestigial organs can be surgically removed with no injury to the body, the organs no longer serve a purpose. They are "useless vestiges" from a former time.

The appendix is often said to be a good example of such an organ. The 2003 *Encyclopedia Britannica* describes the appendix as "a vestigial hollow tube attached to the cecum."[5] Likewise the 2003 *Columbia Encyclopedia* says the appendix "has no function in people and is considered a vestigial remnant of some previous organ or structure, having a digestive function, that became unnecessary to people in their evolutionary progress."[6] In similar fashion, the 2003 *Encarta Encyclopedia* notes that "many scientists believe that the human appendix at one time served a useful purpose that has gradually been lost through evolution."[7] This view is shared by evolutionist Ernst Mayr, who suggests that when such organs "lose their function owing to a shift in lifestyle, they are no longer protected by natural selection and are gradually deconstructed." However, such organs "are informative by showing the previous course of evolution."[8]

Evolutionists are again guilty of making vast and unwarranted assumptions. To begin, organs that are presently categorized as "vestigial" may serve a purpose that is yet unknown to science.[9] Scientists are not infallible and are making new discoveries and revising older theories all the time. Significantly, scientists used to categorize about 180 organs as "vestigial" (an evolutionary scientist who testified at the famous 1925 Tennessee Scopes Trial made this claim[10]). Included were the thyroid gland, the thymus, the pineal gland, the tonsils, the coccyx, the ear muscles, and the appendix.[11] Today, however, because scientists have discovered functional uses for these organs, the list has now dwindled to between zero and six, depending on who you talk to.[12] For this reason, many scientists don't take vestigial arguments seriously anymore, though the vestigial argument for evolution still shows up in textbooks, college lectures, and major encyclopedias. For the record,

- The pineal gland, once categorized as vestigial, is an endocrine gland that triggers growth cycles and sexual development through the secretion of a hormone called melatonin.[13]

- The thymus, once categorized as vestigial, relates to the body's immune system.

- The thyroid gland, once categorized as vestigial, secretes hormones related to proper metabolism and growth.

- The coccyx (tailbone), once categorized as vestigial (and thought to point to a tail in human ancestors), serves the vital purpose of being a critical point of muscle attachment necessary for an upright posture.[14]

- The appendix, once categorized as vestigial, is a part of the immune system that contains antibodies, thus playing a role in preventing disease, especially in the intestines, and apparently more so for young children than adults. One professor of zoology, for example, now says the appendix may be "a lymphoid organ which acts as a reservoir of antibody producing cells."[15]

What about the common evolutionist argument that vestigial organs can be removed from the human body without apparent loss? The reality is that medical specialists may not yet be aware of some kinds of loss. If an organ is removed and the person remains alive, that does not prove the body has no need for the organ. The person may indeed remain alive, but he may not live as optimally as he would have if the organ remained in his body. Further, medical specialists postulate that if an organ is removed from the body, another organ in the body may compensate for its loss. But this compensation should not be taken to mean that the removed organ served no useful purpose. Yet further, some organs—such as tonsils—may be more important in early childhood than in adulthood (for example, they may help young children ward off disease).[16]

I strongly believe all these organs serve a purpose. But even if some organs *were* useless and "leftover" from an earlier period of humanity, they would be examples of microevolution (evolution within specific species), not macroevolution (evolution of one species into another). If the species of man microevolved, some of these organs may have become less important. But this certainly offers no support for the naturalistic evolution of simple life-forms into complex life-forms.

One further point bears mentioning. If evolution were true, we would expect to see not only a loss of some organs ("devolution," involving the so-called vestigial organs) but also the development of some *new* organs. The absence of such new organs would seem to argue against the evolutionary view that humans are increasingly moving toward some optimal design.[17]

Answering Arguments for the Recapitulation Theory

Evolutionists in the past have argued that as an embryo develops within the womb, it repeats *(recapitulates)* the entire evolutionary history of its species. So, at various stages in embryonic development, a human may appear as a single-celled marine organism, a worm with a pulsating heart, a fish with gill slits, an amphibian, a mammal (with a remnant of a tail), and finally a human being. The human embryo supposedly retains "vestiges" of its previous evolution by recapitulating its major evolutionary stages.

Sometimes the theory is summed up in the phrase, "ontogeny recapitulates phylogeny."[18] Allow me to translate these strange-sounding words for you.

- *Ontogeny* refers to embryonic development.

- *Phylogeny* refers to evolutionary development.

- Therefore, the phrase simply means that embryonic development recapitulates (or repeats) evolutionary development.

Tragically, many abortion clinics across the country have used the recapitulation theory to ease the guilt of young girls having abortions. They tell the girls that the embryo is now in the fish stage, so they don't need to worry about killing a human baby.[19] Who knows how many millions of innocent babies have been slaughtered while doctors use the recapitulation theory to assuage guilt.

The idea that the embryo recapitulates its evolutionary history within the womb has certainly been widely disseminated among the masses.

- The *Reader's Digest Book of Facts* reports the "fact" that the human embryo recapitulates its evolutionary history, including developing gill slits like a fish and a tail.[20]

- Dr. Spock, of baby and child development fame, taught this theory (including the idea that the embryo develops gill slits).[21]

- Dr. Ernst Mayr, influential evolutionist who has been hailed as the "Darwin of the twentieth century" and is Professor Emeritus of zoology at Harvard University, argues that an early human embryo is similar not only to dogs, cows, and mice, but also to reptiles, amphibians, and fishes.[22]

- Carl Sagan, once hailed as the smartest man in America, said the following in the widely distributed *Parade Magazine*:

> By the third week, around the time of the first missed menstrual period, the forming embryo is about 2 millimeters long and is developing various body parts. But it looks a little like a segmented worm. By the end of the fourth week, it's approximately 5 millimeters (about 1/5 inch) long. It's recognizable as a vertebrate, its tube-shaped heart is beginning to beat, something like the gill-arches of a fish or an amphibian have become conspicuous, and there is a pronounced tail. It looks something like a newt or a tadpole. This is the end of the first month after conception. By the fifth week, the gross divisions of the brain can be distinguished. What will later develop into eyes is apparent, and little buds appear—on their way to becoming arms and legs. By the sixth week, the embryo is 13 millimeters (about 1/2 inch) long. The eyes are still on the side of the head, as in most animals, and the reptilian face

has connected slits where the mouth and nose eventually will be. By the end of the seventh week, the tail is almost gone, and sexual characteristics can be discerned (although both sexes look female). The face is mammalian, but somewhat pig-like. By the end of the eighth week, the face resembles a primate, but is still not quite human.[23]

This description of the embryo is undoubtedly based on the recapitulation theory. Sadly, Sagan set forth this description of the human embryo in his attempt to justify women having abortions. Many no doubt found Sagan's line of argument quite convincing. I know that students at the university level have found it convincing.

I read one account of a student taking a zoology course at a respected university where the recapitulation theory was being taught. He commented that the presentation was spun in such an effective way that he walked away from the course wondering how anyone could rationally deny that evolution was true. He found that the idea strongly challenged his Christian beliefs. Not until five years later did he discover that by the mid-twentieth century, *no informed embryologist accepted the recapitulation theory as legitimate.*[24] That men like Dr. Spock and Dr. Sagan espoused such ideas is surprising.

From a historical perspective, Charles Darwin firmly believed that embryonic similarities would support his claims. It was sometime later that biologist Ernst Haeckel—a professor of zoology who was Darwin's biggest supporter and promoter in Germany[25]—made drawings of embryos of various species that showed amazing similarity. This was hailed as powerful new evidence for evolution.

Unfortunately for evolutionists, and to the great embarrassment of evolutionists who earlier hailed this discovery, Haeckel's drawings were proven to be fraudulent by other contemporary scientists. He changed other scientists' drawings of human and dog embryos, making their resemblance much closer and masking their dissimilarities.[26] He also misrepresented the stage and age of the embryos.[27]

Though we have known for a long time that Haeckel's drawings were bogus (one recent evolutionist claims they were just "somewhat doctored"[28]), the great magnitude of his deception has only recently come to light. Michael Richardson, embryologist at St. George's Hospital Medical School, London, wrote an article for *Anatomy and Embryology* journal. In the article, he noted that Haeckel's drawings had always raised a red flag in his mind because they didn't match his own research on the subject. As a responsible scientist, he assembled a team of experts to examine and photograph embryos from a wide variety of vertebrate species at a stage comparable to that depicted by Haeckel.[29] Richardson and his team yielded findings so different from Haeckel's drawings that they concluded Haeckel couldn't have been dealing with real specimens. They note that Haeckel's drawings not only added and deleted certain features but also skewed the scale of the drawings to emphasize similarity among species.[30] In a newspaper interview, Richardson commented:

> This is one of the worst cases of scientific fraud. It's shocking to find that somebody one thought was a great scientist was deliberately misleading. It makes me angry.... What he [Haeckel] did was to take a human embryo and copy it, pretending that the salamander and the pig and all the others looked the same at the same stage of development. They don't.... These are fakes.[31]

Haeckel's drawings constitute *zero* proof for evolution. Despite the revelation of this fraud, however, Haeckel's bogus drawings even today continue to appear in biology and evolution textbooks, and they also surface during college and university zoology lectures.[32] Prominent evolutionist Stephen Jay Gould—who says that knowledgeable biologists abandoned this idea some fifty years ago (Sagan should have known better)—says that textbook writers are not always experts in all disciplines and often have a tendency to overly depend on previous textbooks. Misinformation has thus been passed on generation by generation since the time of Haeckel. Gould thus laments that we should be "astonished and ashamed by the century of mindless recycling that has led to the persistence of these drawings in a large number, if not a majority, of modern textbooks."[33] (One scholar counted 50 recent biology textbooks still using Haeckel's bogus drawings uncritically.[34])

Aside from this rank deception, allow me to emphasize that the human embryo never develops gill slits like a fish. Indeed, what evolutionists take to be gill slits has virtually nothing to do with breathing, for the baby takes its oxygen directly from the mother's blood via the umbilical cord.[35] It therefore never goes through a "fish stage." The markings on the human embryo that are taken to be gill slits by evolutionists are actually "pharyngeal clefts" or pouches which eventually develop into the thymus gland, parathyroid glands, and middle ear canals[36]—in perfect accord with the human DNA created by the Creator.

Such evolutionary stages in the embryo are genetically impossible. Indeed, at every stage of development, human DNA ensures the embryo is human. Human DNA produces humans (reproducing after its kind), fish DNA produces fish (reproducing after its kind), and reptile DNA produces reptiles (reproducing after its kind). Human DNA is not fish DNA, nor is it reptile DNA. The DNA of each species has been programmed by the Creator to reproduce only after its kind.

What Can We Conclude?

In this chapter we have seen that

- Similar anatomy does not prove that one animal evolved from another. Rather, such similarity is due to the fact that all animals come from the hand of the same (divine) Designer, who gave creatures similar features (eyes, noses, ears, lungs, and the like) so that they could optimally live in a similar environment.

- The "vestigial organ" theory has been scientifically invalidated since the organs formerly categorized as vestigial have been systematically discovered to have useful functions. In view of this, the theory should be excised from college textbooks and popular encyclopedias and should no longer be taught in zoology lectures.

- The recapitulation theory is scientifically invalidated and based on bogus research, and should therefore be excised from college textbooks and should no longer be taught in zoology lectures.

The Universe Is Intelligently Designed

Long before the Jodie Foster movie came out, I remember reading the late Carl Sagan's book *Contact*. I was fascinated with the idea that scientists affiliated with SETI (the Search for ExtraTerrestrial Intelligence) used powerful radio telescopes to probe into deep space, listening for radio signals that might give a hint of life out there.

SETI scientists listen for signals between 1000 and 3000 megahertz, where natural background static is at a minimum. These scientists filter out certain radio emissions caused by physical processes so they can better detect faint signals from deep space.

If there were intelligent extraterrestrials out there, what would tip the scientists off that an intelligence was involved in a particular radio signal? One such evidence would be a signal that contained a series of prime numbers (numbers that are divisible only by themselves and the number 1). Such a series of numbers would be impossible to account for without an intelligent source. Of course, so far—despite many years of effort and millions of dollars spent—SETI scientists have come up empty. No prime numbers. No intelligent messages from space.

The point is that scientists and investigators refer to a "sign of intelligence." Certain factors, when scientifically evaluated, show beyond reasonable doubt the presence of an intelligence.

Today, various job professions and even whole industries seek for clues of "intelligent design" and intentionality—that is, clues that indicate that an intelligent being intentionally engaged in a particular action and that it wasn't a chance occurrence.[1] Consider, for example, a crime scene investigator (CSI). If such an investigator comes upon a gruesome scene in which the smashed remains of a human being are mixed with the still-smoldering remains of a meteor, he would conclude this was a chance event. He would dismiss any possibility of this unlucky person being intentionally murdered by another person. However, if the investigator came upon a scene where a person had bullet holes in him and his wallet was missing, he would see clear signs of intentionality. He would know another person was involved, and the police would immediately begin searching for the culprit. The question that is always before the mind of a crime scene investigator is, Was this person's demise by design or by accident?

Certainly insurance companies are interested in whether a person's death was by design or by accident. During the writing of this chapter, I saw a television report of a case involving possible insurance fraud. A woman who had a large life insurance policy was dead, and the circumstances surrounding her death were highly suspect. The question investigators seek an answer for is, Did this lady die by accident, or was design involved by the beneficiary of the life insurance policy?

Other fields that look for signs of intelligence or intentionality include archaeology (for example, the inscriptions on the Rosetta Stone), cryptography (in which random signals are distinguished from those that may carry encoded messages), and copyright offices (who seek to determine whether someone purposefully plagiarized a preexisting work). The reality is that in many cases, we can detect signs of intelligence by the effects left behind.[2]

For example, I remember the first time I traveled through South Dakota and saw the image of four presidents chiseled into a granite cliff on a mountainside. The purposeful design in this giant rock is unmistakable. No one seeing this sight would conclude that wind or rain erosion caused it.[3] Such erosion might have caused the Grand Canyon but not Mount Rushmore. Intelligent artistry is obvious in this case.

Likewise, if you look up at the sky during the day and see the words, "Free Concert in the Park Tonight," you can assume that these words were not caused by random clouds but were spelled out by a skywriter. Clearly, such words indicate intelligent design at work.

This leads me to the primary point I want to make. Just as evidence shows crime scene investigators, archaeologists, cryptographers, copyright offices, and people who see words in the sky that an intelligent being was involved, so the universe gives us evidence of an intelligent being. In other words, the world gives us clear evidence that an intelligent being intentionally brought our universe into existence and that the universe was not the result of random chance or a cosmic accident. Such evidence serves as the primary focus of a field that has come to be known as "intelligent design."

The relevance of this field is obvious. An intelligent Designer is at the heart of creationism. Accidental development is at the heart of evolutionism. Hence, as William Dembski says, "Whence cometh the order of the world?" has become one of the most important questions of our time.[4]

From a statistical perspective, most people in the United States do not believe that the Darwinian mechanism of chance variations and natural selection can account for the wide biological diversity of life on this planet. Despite the fact that evolutionary theory continues to be taught in school and continues to be a media favorite on news programs and in newspapers, the majority of the public has simply not bought it. Many people seem to intuitively know that an intelligent Designer is behind our universe.[5] The only other option is to believe that somehow, life emerged from nonlife and eventually evolved into complex life-forms (like humans)—an idea that stretches all credulity.

Creationists Phillip Johnson and Hugh Ross speak of a God who left His fingerprints all over the creation.[6] William Dembski speaks of a God who has left His footprints throughout the creation.[7] Intelligent design theorists are finding evidence for these fingerprints and footprints. To me, this is exciting. Whether you are a young-earth creationist or an old-earth creationist, we can all unite together in pointing to the evidence that God has had His hands all over this creation and has left us plenty of evidence attesting to this fact.

The Historical Backdrop: The Rise and Fall of William Paley

Perhaps the most oft-repeated design argument in Christian history is that of William Paley (1743–1805), a proponent of "natural theology." Paley suggested that if we should find a watch in a field, the assumption would be that an intelligent designer created that watch. His argument goes this way:

> In crossing a heath [grassland or pasture], suppose I pitched my foot against a stone, and were asked how the stone came to be there; I might possibly answer, that, for anything I knew to the contrary, it had lain there forever.... But suppose I had found a watch on the ground, and it should be inquired how the watch happened to be in that place.... The inference, we think, is inevitable—the watch must have had a maker: that there must have existed, at some time, and at some

place or other, an artificer [craftsman] or artificers, who formed it for the purpose which we find it actually to answer; who comprehended its construction, and designed its use.[8]

Paley argued that just as we see evidence for an intelligent designer in the making of a watch, we see evidence for an intelligent Designer in the universe. Science, during Paley's era, was thus viewed as supportive of theism (belief in a personal Creator-God). Because one could observe wonderful adaptations in the world of nature (such as polar bears developing thicker coats to survive the cold) as well as evidences for rationality, power, and benevolence, one could infer the existence of a benevolent and powerful Designer. One could, Paley thought, construct a theology from the world of nature—"natural theology."[9]

Enter Charles Darwin. As soon as evolutionary theory exploded on the scene through the publication of Darwin's *On the Origin of Species,* Paley's design argument was promptly issued out the back door. Darwin convincingly argued that all the evidences for adaptation in the world of nature were actually just examples of mechanical and purposeless natural selection, based entirely on random variations. He saw no evidence for a benevolent and powerful Designer behind it all, "no evidence of beneficent design in the details."[10] Paley, of course, did not have the scientific evidence for intelligent design that modern design theorists have, so his natural theology was virtually overwhelmed by the tidal wave of Darwinism and its emphasis on natural selection.

However, when Darwin came up with his theory on natural selection, he was acutely aware of its vulnerability. In his book *On the Origin of Species*, he conceded that "if it could be demonstrated that any complex organ existed which could not possibly have been formed by numerous, successive, slight modifications, my theory would absolutely break down."[11]

Understanding Irreducible Complexity

The type of organ that would undo Darwin's theory is one that is "irreducibly complex." According to Lehigh University biochemist Michael Behe, an irreducibly complex system is "a single system which is composed of several well-matched, interacting parts that contribute to the basic function, and where the removal of any one of the parts causes the system to effectively cease functioning."[12] In such a system, several components interact with each other, and if any single component is missing from the system, it no longer operates correctly.[13]

Behe suggests that a good example of an irreducibly complex system is a common mechanical mousetrap.[14] A mousetrap has a number of components that are necessary to its functioning, and if any component of the trap is missing, it no longer functions correctly.[15] All its pieces have to be in place to actually catch a mouse.[16] If it's missing a spring, a hammer, or platform, for example, it will not work. It is irreducibly complex. Likewise, some bodily organs and parts—such as the human eye and a bird's wing—involve a variety of interacting components ordered in such a way that they accomplish a function beyond the individual components. They are irreducibly complex and give evidence of intelligent design.[17]

The Irreducibly Complex Eye

One of the best examples of a bodily organ that is irreducibly complex is the eye.[18] Charles Darwin himself dealt with the eye in a chapter called "Organs of Extreme Perfection and Complication" in *On the Origin of Species*. He was no doubt hoping to deflect criticism from mid-nineteenth century biologists who would argue that the eye in all its complexity could not have come about gradually through natural selection. In his book, Darwin conceded that he was unsure how the eye evolved. He suggested that in view of the wide variety of eyes seen in modern organisms (some just detect light, others can focus on objects), there may have been a gradual evolutionary pathway that began with a light-sensitive patch of skin to an eye that could focus.[19] His basic contention was that the eye in its earliest development must have been beneficial to the organism in some small way (heightening its survival rate against predatory animals) so that natural selection maintained and continued to develop it in future generations of that organism.[20] This line of argument seemed to keep some of the critics at bay—at least for the time being.

Today, however, all of this seems like wishful thinking.[21] The more we study the eye, the greater the difficulty of believing that the eye could ever have come about as a result of natural selection. A piece-by-piece development of this incredibly complex organ—resulting from infinitesimally small Darwinian improvements over an unimaginably long period of time, requiring untold thousands of random positive mutations—requires far more faith than the creationist position.

Consider the following technical description of the eye:

> The essential parts of the eye are enclosed in a tough outer coat, the sclerotic, to which the muscles moving it are attached, and which in front changes into the transparent cornea. A little way back of the cornea, the crystalline lens is suspended, dividing the eye into two unequal cavities, a smaller one in front filled with a watery fluid, the aqueous humor, and larger one behind filled with a clear jelly, the vitreous humor. The sclerotic is lined with a highly pigmented membrane, the choroid, and this in turn is lined in the back half of the eyeball with the nearly transparent retina, in which the fibers of the optic nerve ramify. The choroid in front is continuous with the iris, which has a contractile opening in the center, the pupil, admitting light to the lens which brings the rays to a focus and forms an image

upon the retina, where the light, falling upon delicate
structures called rods and cones, causes them to stim-
ulate the fibers of the optic nerve to transmit visual
impressions to the brain.[22]

I do not know what strikes your mind as you read this
description. But to me, the idea that the eye evolved by random
processes is beyond credulity. The description sounds like an
incredibly knowledgeable engineer planned the eye from beginning to end. Certainly the ability of the eye to focus on different objects at different distances alone is a complex procedure
that seems impossible to explain by natural selection. As well,
the ability of the eye to work in perfect and instant synergistic
harmony with the brain to facilitate seeing also seems an impossible task for natural selection to have accomplished.

Against evolutionary theory, Phillip Johnson observes that
the initial steps toward a new bodily function such as seeing
with an eye would provide virtually *no advantage* to an animal
unless the various parts of the eye required for seeing appeared
at the same time.[23] And if the initial steps toward a new bodily
function provided no advantage, one must assume natural selection would weed such initial steps out of the body. Keep in
mind that natural selection is purposeless and unguided and
cannot know the end result of these initial steps. How would
the various parts of the eye know how to assemble themselves
over a very long period of time in order to attain the function
of seeing?

Understandably, Darwin once commented that contemplating the complexity of the eye gave him "a cold shudder."[24]
But it is not the eye alone that should give Darwin a shudder,
for indeed, the bodies of human beings and various animals are
loaded with similar complex organs that give every evidence of
design. Another good example is the wing.

The Irreducibly Complex Wing

How did the wing evolve? Evolutionists try to argue that the body appendage (a small flap or web) that would one day become a wing must have served some useful purpose for the initial animal so that natural selection preserved it for future generations. Richard Dawkins suggests that perhaps the small flap helped the animal to jump farther than it could before or perhaps catch some air to help it to avoid breaking its neck in the event of a fall.[25] Whatever the purpose, it was allegedly enough—even though slight at the beginning—to give the creature an advantage in its fight for survival. As long periods of time passed, the flap or web supposedly developed so that flight eventually became possible.

Again, this seems to be wishful thinking. John Whitcomb observes that even if a creature produced such an appendage (a web or a flap), natural selection would likely weed it out as a useless body part long before the animal had the capability of flying. The problem is that mutations only bring about one tiny change at a time, and the development of a complex body part like a wing would require untold thousands of random positive mutations. How would natural selection, at each minimal step along the way, know whether to keep each small mutational change or breed it out of the species? How would natural selection recognize the worth of a single mutation during a long process of multiple mutations, awaiting the eventual arrival of a complex body part like a wing?[26]

Dawkins' explanation is unconvincing. The initial small web would have likely been so small and insignificant that it would not have sufficient aerodynamic qualities to catch enough air to break a fall or enable an animal to jump farther. And growing a small web or flap is not all that is required to fly. Indeed, both the bodily structure of the entire animal (such as developing new, highly coordinated muscles on the side of the body) and the internal instincts of the (ground) animal must change in order for it to fly.[27] In view of all the variables involved, natural selection simply cannot account for the origin of the wing.

Molecular Machines

The term "black box" is a scientific phrase used to describe a system that does interesting things but that no one can explain.[28] (To many laypeople, the computer is like a black box because it does interesting things, but we have no idea how it works on the inside.[29]) The workings of the system remain utterly mysterious, for no one can peer into the black box, or if they can, they do not comprehend what they see. The cell was a black box for Charles Darwin and nineteenth-century biologists, for they could not comprehend how it worked. Darwinism emerged when little scientific knowledge existed about the inner workings of the cell. However, now that scientists have closely examined the cellular black box, the fictional nature of Darwinism has become apparent.[30]

Nineteenth-century biologists believed the cell was composed of simple protoplasm.[31] Today, however, we have learned that the cell contains ultrasophisticated molecular machines.[32] And in view of the complexity of molecular life, the key question has become, Can Darwinism account for this complexity? As noted previously, Darwin himself said that if a complex organ existed that could not have been formed by "numerous, successive, slight modifications," then his theory would break down. Many people today believe that the existence of complex, information-rich structures at the molecular level cannot be explained by Darwinism and calls for the existence of an intelligent Designer.[33]

What kinds of complexity do we witness at the molecular level? Dembski observes that we witness high-tech molecular systems that include such hallmarks as "information storage and transfer; functioning codes; sorting and delivery systems; self-regulation and feedback loops; signal transduction circuitry; and everywhere, complex arrangements of mutually-interdependent and well fitted parts that work in concert to perform a function."[34] Sounds complicated. But Dembski's point is that the complexity that we witness at the molecular level is every bit as "high-tech" as some of the high-tech electronic gadgets created by man. These ultrasophisticated molecular machines show just as much evidence of design as do modern computers.[35] Observations at the molecular level virtually beg for an explanation—an explanation that Darwinism cannot provide.[36]

In an interview with NPR News, Michael Behe explained the complexity of cells using transportation metaphors:

> What we've discovered in a cell in the past half-century or so are quite literally molecular machines, machines of enormous complexity. There are little machines in the cell that act as trucks and buses that take supplies from one side of the cell to the other. And they use little signposts, and there are garage doors that open and shut to let the supplies into various compartments.[37]

Behe quite convincingly demonstrates complexity at the molecular level with his discussion of the ion-powered rotary engines that turn the whip-like flagella of certain bacteria. He notes that this complex machinery includes such components as a rotor, a stator, O-rings, bushings, and a driveshaft.[38] He argues that since multiple independent protein parts are necessary in order for this molecular mechanism to function—and since the absence of any single component of this mechanism would cause it not to function—gradualistic natural selection (through multiple intermediate stages over a long period of time) could never explain the emergence of such mechanisms. With a cell it is "all or nothing."[39] The only explanation that makes sense is that an intelligent Designer is behind such irreducibly complex mechanisms. Such molecular mechanisms must have been created fully formed, with all parts in place, or else they would not function.

The Information in DNA

DNA—an abbreviation for *deoxyribonucleic acid*—carries genetic information in the cell and is capable of self-replication. The volume of information contained in DNA absolutely staggers the mind. As Richard Dawkins put it, "There is enough information capacity in a single human cell to store the *Encyclopedia Britannica*, all 30 volumes of it, three or four times over."[40] Put another way, "The amount of information that could be stored in a pinhead's volume of DNA is equivalent to a pile of paperback books 500 times as tall as the distance from Earth to the Moon, each with a different, yet specific content."[41] The relevance to the current debate is obvious. Where did this staggering amount of information—much like computer software code inside a computer[42]—come from? Naturalistic evolution certainly cannot explain it.[43] All the evidence points to the existence of a divine programmer.

To expand on the software analogy, Microsoft founder Bill Gates says that "DNA is like a computer program, but far, far more advanced than any software we've ever created."[44] Computer programs do not write themselves. A programmer is always involved. Even if you provide plenty of time, a computer program still cannot write itself. The same is true regarding the information in DNA. Somebody had to program that information into DNA.

I may not have seen the computer programmer write the word processing software I am now using to write this book, but I have no doubt that the programmer exists.[45] In the same way, I may not have seen the divine Designer do His work of programming information into DNA, but I have no doubt that an intelligent Mind was involved in the process.

Design Theory: Contingency, Complexity, and Specification

So far in this chapter, I have addressed irreducibly complex organs like the eye and wing, as well as the complexity that we witness at the molecular level and the staggering volume of information in DNA. Now I want to shift attention to the actual scientific theory that enables us to detect design in the universe. Such a scientific theory is important, for the existence of an intelligent Designer is not postulated by design theorists as a religious viewpoint (they do not even explicitly identify the Designer as God, though that is the obvious implied conclusion).[46] Intelligent design theory holds that an intelligent cause is empirically detectable by using a well-defined scientific method. This method focuses on *contingency*, *complexity*, and *specification*. These may sound like big words, but this theory is not hard to grasp.

In a capsule, if something were designed, we would expect to see evidence of *contingency*, meaning it did not result from an automatic, unintelligent process (like natural selection). If something were designed, we would expect to see evidence that it was *complex* enough (with many interacting working parts) that random chance processes alone would not be able to cause its existence. If something were designed, we would also expect to see evidence of *specificity*—a detailed, precise pattern commonly associated with intelligent causes.[47]

We might illustrate "specified complexity" this way:

- The letter "A" is specified without being complex.

- The random sequence of letters "AQXRBZN" is complex without being specified.

- The sentence "HOUSTON, WE HAVE A PROBLEM!" is both complex and specified. *Specified complexity is our means of empirically detecting design in the universe.*[48]

Many scholars from the fields of science and philosophy see evidences of specified complexity in our universe, which is perfectly balanced to support life. Jimmy H. Davis and Harry L. Poe explain that specified complexity is evident in "the universe's coincidences of having the right atoms, the right molecules, enough time, and enough space for life to occur." They also see specified complexity "in the earth's coincidences of the right galaxy type, the location in the galaxy, the type of star, the earth's distance from the sun, the location of Jupiter, the size of the moon, and the composition of the earth."[49] Just as a Shakespearean sonnet is both complex and specified, so different features of our universe are complex and specified.

Our universe is finely tuned for the possibility of human life.[50] Numerous highly improbable factors have to be precisely in place in a balanced fashion for the survival of life on earth. Without any one of these factors, life would not be possible. As one scholar put it, "almost everything about the basic structure of the universe...is balanced on a razor's edge for life to occur."[51] Indeed, "one could think of the initial conditions of the universe and the fundamental parameters of physics as a dart board that fills the whole galaxy, and the conditions necessary for life to exist as a small one-foot wide target: unless the dart hits the target, life would be impossible."[52] Life has emerged on earth because the dart in fact "hit the target."

To give an illustration of one aspect of this fine-tuning, if the rate of expansion of our universe were any different, life on earth would not be possible.[53] As Hugh Ross explains it,

> If the universe expanded too rapidly, matter would disperse so efficiently that none of it would clump enough to form galaxies. If no galaxies form, no stars will form. If no stars form, no planets will form. If no planets form, there's no place for life. On the other hand, if the universe expanded too slowly, matter would

clump so effectively that all of it, the whole universe
in fact, would collapse into a super dense lump before
any solar-type stars could form.[54]

Further, if the strength of gravitational or electromagnetic
attraction were different, life on earth would not be possible.[55]
If our moon were significantly larger, the gravitational pull of
the moon would be greater, and this would cause tidal waves
to engulf the land.[56] Likewise, if earth had more than one moon,
the oceans would be unstable. If earth were significantly closer
to the sun, the heat would increase such that life could not
survive on earth. Our atmosphere has just enough oxygen for
creatures to be able to breathe. In short, everything about our
earth and the universe seems tailor-made for the existence of
human life (and other life-forms).

Are these and a host of other similar factors the result of a
random cosmic coincidence, or was an intelligent Designer
involved? Many today believe the evidence for an intelligent
Designer is undeniable, for the specified complexity evident in
our universe is undeniable.

- Robert Jastrow, author of *God and the Astronomers*, writes:
  "If the universe had not been made with the most exact-
  ing precision we could never have come into existence.
  It is my view that these circumstances indicate the
  universe was created for man to live in."[57]

- Astronomer Frederick Hoyle came to the conclusion that
  "a superintellect has monkeyed with physics, as well as
  with chemistry and biology."[58] Indeed, a superintellect
  has fine-tuned our universe for the existence of life.

- Astronomer George Greenstein, after observing the apparent design in the universe, asked if it is possible that we

have "stumbled upon scientific proof for the existence of a Supreme Being."[59]

In view of the deluge of evidence for intelligent design in the universe, naturalism as a philosophy is in freefall.[60] "Freefall" is defined by the *American Heritage Dictionary* as "rapid uncontrolled decline."[61] This decline is obvious in the conclusion of biophysicist Dean Kenyon, who suggests that the more scientists learn about molecular biology and the "chemical details of life," the less likely is a "strictly naturalistic" explanation for origins.[62] An increasing number of scientists are concluding that the universe *appears* to be designed because it *is* designed.[63]

Evolutionist Objections to Intelligent Design Can Be Intelligently Answered

A theory that strongly challenges evolution and the naturalistic philosophy that undergirds it will understandably receive a chorus of objections from the evolutionist camp. The more common objections include (1) intelligent design gives up on science, (2) intelligent design is unscientific, (3) the need for design improvements disproves a divine intelligent Designer, (4) the problem of evil disproves a divine intelligent Designer, and (5) scientific theories cannot involve miracles. Interestingly, some young-earth creationists have also voiced a few objections.[1] In what follows I will briefly address these objections.

Intelligent Design Gives Up on Science

The Objection. Hardline evolutionists claim that intelligent design theory gives up on science. They say that theories like intelligent design "stifle further inquiry by attributing what may not yet be understood to an unknowable cause."[2] As one physicist put it, "intelligent design is a shorthand for interjecting God," and God should not be interjected in *any* scientific studies.[3]

As well, many scientists who are theists believe that any suggested design theory should be kept separate and distinct from science, even though they themselves may believe in a Designer. The primary concern is that if they are not kept separate, researchers may be tempted to insert the "Designer solution" at any point in scientific inquiry where no scientific answer is readily apparent. A "God of the gaps" fills in the holes of missing scientific information.[4]

Answering the Objection. Intelligent design theorists do not believe in intelligent design simply because of "gaps" in our knowledge. Rather, they believe in intelligent design because evidence for design is empirically detectable by using a well-defined scientific method that focuses on contingency, complexity, and specification (see chapter 8).[5] Just as a forensic detective would infer an intelligent cause of a crime he was investigating by using scientific techniques, so design can be rationally inferred in the universe by using scientific techniques. Intelligent design theory is not dependent upon religious views.

In a lecture delivered at the American Museum of Natural History, Michael Behe commented:

> Some of my critics have said that design is a religious conclusion, but I disagree. I think it is wholly empirical, that is, the conclusion of design is based on the physical evidence along with an appreciation for how we come to a conclusion of design. To illustrate how we come to a conclusion of design, let's look at the following. [At this point a cartoon slide is shown to the audience depicting an explorer caught by a roped foot trap.] This is a *Far Side* cartoon by Gary Larson showing a troop of jungle explorers, and the lead explorer has been strung up and skewered. Now, everyone in this room looks at this cartoon and you immediately realize that the trap was designed. But how do you know that? How do you know the trap was designed? Is it a religious conclusion? Probably not. You know it's designed because you see a number of very

> specific parts acting together to perform a function;
> you see something like irreducible complexity or spec-
> ified complexity.[6]

Instead of "giving up" on science, intelligent design theorists say they thoroughly utilize scientific methodology. Far from
being grounded in a gap in knowledge, intelligent design theory
has grown out of our scientific knowledge of irreducibly complex
cells and organs.

Another point bears mentioning. Turning the tables on
evolutionists, Behe urges, "We have to watch out that we don't
have what we might call, say, a naturalism of the gaps as well.
And that is the idea that what we can't explain today, well, we
know that natural unguided processes did it somehow, but we'll
figure how that was done later."[7] *Touché!*

Intelligent Design Is Unscientific

The Objection. Some evolutionists argue against intelligent
design theory by pointing out that results cannot be measured,
counted, repeated, and/or tested. If one cannot measure, count,
repeat, or test results, one cannot be involved in science.[8] One
evolutionist objects, "Their arguments don't lead to anything
that's empirically investigable."[9] Another argues that "the scientific method of testing hypotheses requires observation," and
intelligent design cannot be "demonstrated clearly through a
laboratory test."[10]

Answering the Objection. Repetition is impossible in a number
of areas of scientific study. Many scientists presently believe in
the big bang theory, but this event happened (allegedly) only
once, so no one was there to observe it firsthand, no one was
there to take measurements, and we certainly have no way of
repeating the event in a laboratory so that it can be tested over
and over again. Yet no one balks at including the big bang theory
within the realm of science.

Likewise, simply because we cannot repeat in a laboratory the fossilization process of ancient life-forms does not exclude paleontology from the realm of science. Simply because we cannot repeat the inscription on the Rosetta Stone does not exclude archaeology from the realm of science.[11] Simply because no one observed a so-called extinct common ancestor does not exclude evolution from science. Likewise, simply because we cannot repeat the work of the original intelligent Designer in a laboratory does not exclude intelligent design from science. The reality is that science is far more than repetition.

As for "testability," a scientific testing process includes examining theories against new evidence and theoretical insights. This was how Darwin tested and then dismissed the design arguments of William Paley. In this same sense, Darwin's theory has been tested and found wanting by the new evidence of intelligent design theory.[12]

The Need for Design Improvements Disproves a Divine Intelligent Designer

The Objection. Evolutionists such as Stephen Jay Gould have argued that because certain biological designs fall short of some idealized optimum, they have no divine intelligent Designer behind them.[13] In other words, because we can imagine ways to improve a particular design means the structure in question was not designed. Surely a divine intelligent Designer would have done a better job.

Answering the Objection. This line of argumentation is faulty. I might look at a particular model of a car and think of various ways the car could have a better design, but that does not mean the car itself did not come from the hands of a designer. I might look at the floorplan of a house and decide that the plan could be better in some ways, but that does not mean the floorplan did not come from the hands of an intelligent designer. Biological structures in the universe are no different. Just because someone might imagine how a structure might have had a better design does not mean the structure did not come from an intelligent Designer.

Further, we might think we have a better design in mind for a humanly designed structure, but upon talking to the designer, we might discover some important variables we had not previously considered that cast the design in a different (more favorable) light. For example, I might think that a computer casing would have a better design if it were much smaller. But then the engineer that designed it might inform me that the larger size better accommodates the cooling system for the components in the computer that generate heat. This new information adjusts my thinking so that I now know my idea is not necessarily a better design.

In the same way, we may think we can come up with better designs for molecular structures or for complex organs, but variables may be involved that we know nothing about and that the intelligent Designer is fully aware of. Maybe we do not know as much as we think we do. And besides, how do we know whether our suggested change would actually make a structure better? Introducing a new element might result in some malfunction we had not anticipated.

The Problem of Evil Disproves a Divine Intelligent Designer

The Objection. Perhaps the most weighty objection raised by evolution enthusiasts relates to the existence of evil in the world.[14] In this view, the presence of so much horrible evil in the world proves that the world was not created by an intelligent Designer.[15]

Charles Darwin once said, "I cannot persuade myself that a beneficent and omnipotent God would have designedly created the Ichneumonidae with the express intention of their feeding within the living bodies of caterpillars, or that the cat should play with mice." Darwin thought there was just "too much misery in the world" to accept the idea of design in the universe.[16] His writings reflect an intense philosophical struggle with the problem of pain and evil in the world. The death of his daughter Annie in 1851 further soured him against believing in an intelligent Designer. Darwin's anger and grief over this tragedy played a role in his eventual renouncing of the Christian faith. He struggled with how an omniscient and omnipotent God could allow such bad things to happen to good people.

Answering the Objection. At first glance, this argument may seem convincing. But a look at the facts illustrates that the existence of evil is compatible with the existence of an all-good, all-knowing, and all-powerful Designer. Because this objection comes up so often, and because it is a more potent objection, I will devote more attention to it.

An intelligent design of the universe does not preclude the existence of evil in it. An important beginning point in disarming this objection is to note that evil is simply a perversion of something good that already exists. Evil is not something that has an existence all its own; rather, it is a corruption of that which already exists. Evil is the absence or privation of something good. Rot, for example, can only exist as long as the tree exists. Tooth decay can only exist as long as the tooth exists. Rust on a car and a decaying carcass illustrate the same point. Evil exists as a corruption of something good; it is a privation and does not have essence by itself.[17] Christian philosopher Norman Geisler tells us, "Evil is like a wound in an arm or moth-holes in a garment. It exists only in another but not in itself."[18] Rotting trees, rusting cars, tooth decay, brain cancer—all these are examples of how evil is a corruption of something good.

Understanding evil is one thing. Understanding how such evil can exist in a world created by God is entirely different. The conundrum is a conflict involving three concepts: God's power, God's goodness, and the presence of evil in the world.

Common sense seems to tell us that all three cannot be true at the same time.[19] Solutions to the problem of evil typically involve modifying one or more of these three concepts: Limit God's power, limit God's goodness, or modify the existence of evil (such as calling it an illusion).[20]

Certainly if God made no claims to being good, then the existence of evil would be easier to explain. But God does claim to be good. If God were limited in power so that He were not strong enough to withstand evil, then the existence of evil would be easier to explain. But God does claim to be all-powerful. If evil were just an illusion that had no reality, then the problem would not exist in the first place. But evil is not an illusion. It is real.[21]

Creationists believe the original creation was "very good" (Genesis 1:31). Sin, evil, pain, and death did not exist. Yet today, the world is permeated with sin, evil, pain, and death. What brought it about? Scripture indicates that the turn downward came the moment Adam and Eve used their God-given free wills to choose to disobey God (Genesis 3).

Some people wonder why God didn't create humans in such a way that we would never sin, thus avoiding evil altogether. Wouldn't that be a better design? But such a scenario would mean that we are no longer truly human. We would no longer have the capacity to make choices and to freely love. This scenario would require that God create robots who act only in programmed ways—like one of those chatty dolls with a string in its back that says, "I love you."[22] Christian apologist Paul Little notes that with such a doll "there would never be any hot words, never any conflict, never anything said or done that would make you sad! But who would want that? There would never be any love, either. Love is voluntary. God could have made us like robots, but we would have ceased to be men. God apparently thought it worth the risk of creating us as we are."[23]

Love cannot be programmed; it must be freely expressed. God wanted Adam and all humanity to show love by freely

138 The Creation vs. Evolution Debate

choosing obedience. That is why God gave Adam and all other humans a free will. Geisler is correct in saying that "forced love is rape; and God is not a divine rapist. He will not do anything to coerce their decision."[24] A free choice, however, leaves the possibility of a wrong choice. As J. B. Phillips put it, "Evil is inherent in the risky gift of free will."[25]

In view of the scriptural facts, we may conclude that God's plan had the *potential* for evil when He bestowed upon humans the freedom of choice, but the *actual origin* of evil came as a result of a man who directed his will away from God and toward his own selfish desires.[26] "Whereas God created the *fact* of freedom, humans perform the *acts* of freedom. God made evil *possible;* creatures make it *actual.*"[27] Ever since Adam and Eve made evil actual on that first occasion in the Garden of Eden, a sin nature has been passed on to every man and woman (Romans 5:12; 1 Corinthians 15:22), and with our sin nature we continue to use our free wills to make evil actual (Mark 7:20-23).

The fact that humans used God-given free choice to disobey God did not take God by surprise. C.S. Lewis suggests that God in His omniscience "saw that from a world of free creatures, even though they fell, he could work out...a deeper happiness and a fuller splendor than any world of automata would admit."[28] The theist does not have to claim that our present world is the best of all possible worlds, but it is the best way *to* the best possible world. One Christian scholar writes:

> If God is to both preserve freedom and defeat evil, then this is the best way to do it. Freedom is preserved in that each person makes his own free choice to determine his destiny. Evil is overcome in that, once those who reject God are separated from the others, the decisions of all are made permanent. Those who choose God will be confirmed in it, and sin will cease. Those who reject God are in eternal quarantine and cannot

upset the perfect world that has come about. The ultimate goal of a perfect world with free creatures will
have been achieved, but the way to get there requires
that those who abuse their freedom be cast out.[29]

We must remember that God is not finished yet. Too often
people fall into the trap of thinking that because God has not
dealt with evil yet, He is not dealing with it at all. My former
colleague Walter Martin used to say, "I've read the last chapter
in the book, and we win!" Evil will one day be done away with.
Just because evil is not destroyed right now does not mean it
never will be.

So we see that the existence of evil in the world is compatible with the existence of an all-good and all-powerful God. We
can summarize the facts this way:

1. If God is all-good, He *will* defeat evil.

2. If God is all-powerful, He *can* defeat evil.

3. Evil is *not yet* defeated.

4. Therefore, God *can and will* one day defeat evil.[30]

In view of this, the existence of evil in the world does not
constitute a proof that the world was not intelligently designed.
I can know this just as surely as I can know my house was intelligently designed despite the fact that one of its pipes sprang a
leak. Remember that evil always involves the perversion of something that is good. The divine Designer's creation *was* entirely
good. Simply because free will creatures brought evil into that
good creation does not negate the creation's design.

Scientific Theories Cannot Involve Miracles

The Objection. A final objection that often comes up is that
scientific theories cannot admit the possibility of miracles.

Charles Darwin once said, "I will give absolutely nothing for the theory of natural selection if it requires miraculous additions at any one stage of descent."[31] Darwin's feelings have been echoed by multiple evolutionists and scientists since his time.

Answering the Objection. Earlier in this book, I addressed the issue of naturalism. You will recall that the philosophy of naturalism asserts that the universe operates according to uniform natural causes and that no force outside the universe can intervene in the cosmos. This is where naturalism goes so far astray. In my chapter on naturalism, I provided arguments in favor of the possibility of miracles. Without repeating all that material, allow me to summarize a few critical points.

Creationists do not argue against the idea that a general uniformity exists in the present cosmos. Regularity and order are in the universe because God created it that way. What creationists take exception to is the notion that the universe is a self-contained closed system with absolute laws that are inviolable. Such a position would rule out any involvement of God in the world He created.

Creationists believe the laws of nature are observations of uniformity or constancy in nature. They are not forces which initiate action. They simply describe the way nature behaves when its course is not affected by a superior power. But God is not prohibited from taking action in the world if He so desires.

When a miracle occurs, the laws of nature are not violated but are rather superseded by a higher (supernatural) manifestation of the will of God. The forces of nature are not obliterated or suspended but are only counteracted at a particular point by a superior force. In other words, miracles do not go against the regular laws of cause and effect; they simply have a cause that transcends nature.[32]

Do miracles disrupt any possibility of doing real science by undermining uniformity in the world? As I noted previously, uniformity is in the world because God created the world that way. Miracles are unusual events that involve only a brief super-seding of the natural laws. By definition, they are out of the norm. And unless a norm existed to begin with, miracles would not be possible. Miracles are unusual, not commonplace events. A miracle is a unique event that stands out against the background of ordinary and regular occurrences. The possibility of miracles does not disrupt the possibility of doing real science.

Young-Earth Creationist Criticisms of Intelligent Design

Some young-earth creationists have pointed out that while some Bible-believing Christians are in the intelligent design movement, other Christians in the movement have a much lower view of the Bible, and some in the movement are not even Christians at all.[33] For this reason, some young-earth creation-ists have a friendly but somewhat cautious attitude in associ-ating too closely with them.

Young-earth creationists also point out that the intelligent design movement as a whole declines from explicitly identify-ing the intelligent Designer as God.[34] One design theorist says "that is not part of the argument…. Who or what is a different topic. The identity of the designer is a different question."[35] Young-earth creationists believe intelligent design theorists are evading the obvious. John Morris, a young-earth creationist who heads up the Institute for Creation Research, says: "We support the intelligent design people fully, but we just feel they don't go far enough. The evidence for design is obvious, but we know who the Designer is."[36]

Defining the identity of the intelligent Designer seems an issue of obvious importance in the light of the many compet-ing and conflicting religious viewpoints on how our universe was designed. New Age enthusiasts often argue that benevolent Space Brothers (aliens) from a distant galaxy planted life on earth and enhanced conditions on our planet for the continued exis-tence of life. Scientology—a new religion founded by fiction writer L. Ron Hubbard—argues that the universe was mentally emanated into existence by powerful thetans (godlike beings). Specifically identifying the divine Designer could go a long way in preventing the spread of deviant viewpoints.

To be fair to intelligent design theorists, their agenda has never been religious in nature. Their goal has been to use scientific methodology to empirically detect design in the universe and to scientifically demonstrate that evolution is a notion without foundation in fact. Further, a nonreligious approach (not explicitly identifying the Designer) stands a better chance of being heard in the social and legislative arena. The fact that there are some non-Christians involved in the movement may help deflect charges of religious bias.[37]

In any event, I think that creationist Helen Fryman adds a very nice perspective regarding how we can look at all this. She notes that by showing that evolution is scientifically and mathematically impossible, intelligent design theorists are blasting away at the mountain. Creationists must now build a road over the mountain. Intelligent design theorists have prepared the turf; creationists now need to build on that prepared turf. And in doing so, they need to pave a road that takes people straight to the true divine Creator—God, manifest in human flesh in the person of Jesus Christ.[38]

God: The Purposeful Designer

All in all, I rejoice in the evidences that intelligent design theorists are bringing to the table. While I may personally wish they would go further and explicitly identify the Designer as God, creationists can "take the ball and run with it."

In view of the massive evidence for an intelligent Designer of the universe, and in view of the fact that objections to intelligent design are inconsequential, I have a new appreciation for the words of Psalm 19:1-4:

The heavens declare the glory of God;
    the skies proclaim the work of his hands.
Day after day they pour forth speech;
    night after night they display knowledge.
There is no speech or language
    where their voice is not heard.
Their voice goes out into all the earth,
    their words to the ends of the world.

The "Big Bang" Theory May or May Not Be Compatible with Creationism

The big bang theory holds that 13 to 15 billion years ago, a massive cosmic explosion marked the beginning of the universe. We are told that the universe exploded into existence from a tiny volume smaller than the period at the end of this sentence.[1]

The big bang theory has made quite a "big bang" in the scientific community, and many Christians—more specifically, old-earth creationists—believe it is how God brought the universe into being in the beginning (Genesis 1:1). Young-earth creationists, however, are generally not impressed with the theory and present good reasons (even scientific reasons) for rejecting it. In what follows, I will first describe what many scientists say about the big bang theory and then proceed to summarize how old-earth creationists and young-earth creationists differ in their views on the theory.

The Big Bang Theory

I think I am on safe ground in affirming that a majority of astrophysicists and cosmologists today believe the big bang represents the beginning of our universe. A key component of the big bang theory is the claim by astronomers that galaxies are moving away from the earth at a phenomenal speed. In his book *God and the Astronomers*, Robert Jastrow notes that astronomers Milton Humason and Edwin Hubble, using the 100-inch telescope on Mount Wilson, found that "the most distant galaxy they could observe was retreating from the earth at the extraordinary velocity of 100 million miles an hour."[2] Many have noted that quite a big bang must have caused that kind of velocity. Jastrow believes we are presently witnessing the aftermath of a *gigantic* explosion.[3]

How long ago did this explosion occur? Does this explosion give us a hint as to how old the universe is? Many believe so. Indeed, by retracing the movements of the galaxies and accounting for their expansion speed, we can determine a point where all these galaxies were packed together in a tiny "egg" that was very hot and very dense. "Putting an expanding universe in reverse leads us back to the point where the universe gets smaller and smaller until it vanishes into nothing."[4] Based on such measurements, the universe may be 13 billion years old (some say 15 billion).[5] In this scenario, every star, every planet, every living creature is rooted in events set in motion at the moment of that cosmic explosion so long ago.[6]

Scientists believe that since this big bang explosion, the universe has not only been expanding but has also been cooling. It had a hot beginning; it's been cooling ever since—something that is typical of a large explosion.

Theorists have speculated that specific galaxies with first-generation stars began to emerge about a billion years after the big bang explosion. More recently, however, some scientists believe such stars may have emerged as early as 200 million years after the cosmic explosion.[7] About 12 billion years after the big bang, life allegedly appeared on planet earth.[8]

Edwin Hubble, who postulated that the galaxies are moving away from each other, also postulated that the farther away the galaxies are, the faster they are receding. Scientists use the term "redshift" to describe the experimental finding that suggests this increase in speed. As a galaxy moves away from earth, its color becomes redder, and the degree of color change is supposedly directly proportional to the speed of the galaxy moving away from earth. This effect is called "redshift." Galaxies that are far away from earth manifest this redshift.[9] This is allegedly due to the fact that "stars that move away from an observer emit light of a slightly longer wavelength—the faster they move, the greater the change in the wavelength."[10]

Some big bang advocates offer an analogy that makes the concept more understandable. If a train passes by you and blows its horn, the pitch of the horn goes from high to low. This change in pitch occurs because as the train approaches you, the wavelength of the sound is *compressed*, whereas after it passes you and is moving away from you, the reverse happens, and the soundwaves *expand*, thus lowering the pitch of the horn. In much the same way, the "redshift" in distant galaxies implies they are moving away from us because red is the longest wavelength of visible light, and stars that move away from us emit light of a longer wavelength. The degree of redness may indicate the speed at which the galaxies are moving away from us.[11]

When scientists began grappling with the implications of the big bang theory, many of them were disturbed—even repulsed—to find the theory pointing toward certain Christian themes, such as the idea that the universe had a beginning.[12] Albert Einstein, for example, developed the theory of general relativity, which implied that the universe was expanding, and he was quite annoyed because this implied that the universe must have had a beginning (and a Beginner). This was unpalatable to Einstein's mind, so he came up with a "cosmological constant" to maintain a static universe, thus avoiding the idea that the universe was expanding and had a beginning. When other scientists proved to him that the universe was indeed expanding, he called his "cosmological constant" the biggest blunder of his career.[13] He eventually gave in to the idea that a superior reasoning power must be responsible for bringing the universe into being—though the god he acknowledged is not the personal God of the Bible.

Old-Earth Creationists Embrace the Big Bang

Many Christians—more specifically, old-earth creationists—believe the big bang theory is quite compatible with biblical teaching. These creationists see significance in the fact that the astronomers and cosmologists who discovered and wrote about the big bang theory did not have a religious bias in favor of Christianity and then go looking for scientific support for their view. Rather, these were scientists doing science—with no religious intent—who postulated the big bang theory after evaluating the evidence from deep space. "Despite its religious implications, the Big Bang was a scientific theory that flowed naturally from observational data, not from holy writings or transcendental visions."[14] Without even intending to, scientists may have stumbled upon evidence for God—and this has caused a number of scientists to take a second look at the possibility of a divine Creator.

Robert Jastrow thus speaks of the evidence for the beginning of the universe as a starting point for faith for many people.[15] Astronomer Allan Sandage stated that "contemplating the majesty of the big bang" helped make him "a believer in God, willing to accept that creation could only be explained as a 'miracle.'"[16] Hugh Ross likewise observes that "astronomers who do not draw theistic or deistic conclusions are becoming rare, and even the few dissenters hint that the tide is against them."[17]

Old-earth creationists point out that in view of the law of cause and effect, a big bang explosion necessarily demands someone or something that "pushed the button" and caused the explosion to happen. The event could not have caused itself. Reason demands that whatever caused the universe must be greater than the universe. That cause must be God—who Himself is the uncaused First Cause. As Hebrews 3:4 puts it, "Every house is built by someone, but God is the builder of everything." God, who is beyond time altogether, is the one who brought the space-time universe into being. He is not limited to the space-time dimensions of this universe but is transcendent above it.

Some people suggest that the big bang is part and parcel of the design that God built into the universe.[18] As I noted in the previous chapter, if the rate of expansion of our universe were any different, life on earth would not be possible.[19] If it expanded too rapidly, matter would disperse so fast that it could not clump together to form galaxies (with stars and planets). If the universe expanded too slowly, matter would end up clumping together and collapse into a dense lump before individual stars could form.[20] Apparently, old-earth creationists suggest, the big bang was a very carefully controlled event, providentially designed by God to allow for the formation of galaxies and the survival of life on earth.[21]

This explosion, theorists say, marks the actual beginning of the universe as well as the beginning of time itself. Hebrews 1:2 is sometimes cited regarding the beginning of time, for it tells us that the Father "has spoken to us by his Son, whom he appointed heir of all things, and through whom he made *the universe*" (italics added). The last part of this verse is rendered more literally from the Greek, "through whom he made *the ages*." Likewise, Hebrews 11:3 tells us that "by faith we understand that *the universe* was formed at God's command" (italics added). This is more literally from the Greek, "By faith we understand that *the ages* were formed at God's command."

Scholars have grappled with what the term "ages" may mean here. Bible scholar R.C.H. Lenski says the term means "not merely vast periods of time as mere time, but 'eons' with all that exists as well as all that transpires in them."[22] New Testament scholar F. F. Bruce says that "the whole created universe of space and time is meant."[23] From this verse, theologian John Mac-Arthur concludes that God created not only "the physical earth but also time, space, force, action, and matter."[24]

Church father and philosopher Augustine (A.D. 354–430) held that the universe was not created *in* time, but that time itself was created *along with* the universe.[25] Reformed theologian Louis Berkhof agrees and concludes:

> It would not be correct to assume that time was already in existence when God created the world, and that He at some point in that existing time, called "the beginning," brought forth the universe. The world was created *with* time rather than *in* time. Back of the beginning mentioned in Genesis 1:1 lies a beginningless eternity.[26]

The idea that time had a beginning agrees with modern science. Indeed, Stephen Hawking, author of *A Brief History of Time*, has argued that time must have a beginning.

Scripture not only points to a beginning of time but may also give support to the idea of a big bang explosion. Old-earth creationists typically point to the following verses (note the words I have italicized):

- He alone *stretches out the heavens* and treads on the waves of the sea (Job 9:8).

- He wraps himself in light as with a garment; he *stretches out the heavens* like a tent (Psalms 104:2).

- He sits enthroned above the circle of the earth, and its people are like grasshoppers. He *stretches out the heavens* like a canopy, and spreads them out like a tent to live in (Isaiah 40:22).

- This is what God the LORD says—He who *created the heavens and stretched them out*, who spread out the earth and all that comes out of it, who gives breath to its people, and life to those who walk on it (Isaiah 42:5).

- This is what the LORD says—your redeemer, who formed you in the womb: I am the LORD, who has made all things, who alone *stretched out the heavens*, who spread out the earth by myself (Isaiah 44:24).

- It is I who made the earth and created mankind upon it. My own hands *stretched out the heavens;* I marshaled their starry hosts (Isaiah 45:12).

- My own hand laid the foundations of the earth, and my right hand *spread out the heavens;* when I summon them, they all stand up together (Isaiah 48:13).

- God made the earth by his power; he founded the world by his wisdom and *stretched out the heavens* by his understanding (Jeremiah 10:12).

- He made the earth by his power; he founded the world by his wisdom and *stretched out the heavens* by his understanding (Jeremiah 51:15).

- This is the word of the LORD concerning Israel. The LORD, who *stretches out the heavens*, who lays the foundation of the earth… (Zechariah 12:1).

The phrase "stretched out" in these verses comes from a Hebrew word that carries the idea "spread out," "extend out," to "outspread," or "to extend something outward." In view of these verses, God's "stretching out" of the stars may be a scriptural way of describing the big bang.

Young-Earth Creationists Reject the Big Bang

Not all Christians agree that the big bang theory explains the origins of the universe—especially if this big bang occurred some 13 to 15 billion years ago. I am referring to young-earth creationists, who view the earth as being not billions of years old but rather less than 10,000 years old. On the one hand, some young-earth creationists allow for the possibility that galaxies are moving away from us at high speed and acknowledge that if that is indeed the case, the Scripture verses mentioned previously may be interpreted as going along with this expansion (see also Job 26:7; Isaiah 51:13). But these verses could just as easily refer to a static (non-expanding) universe that God originally spread out (all at once) at the time of the creation.[27]

Young-earth creationists also note some rather serious scientific problems with the idea that the universe is expanding. For example, this expansion is not directly observable but is rather an inference from the observation that light from distant galaxies has a longer wavelength (it is red). In recent years, some have questioned whether this redshift proves that galaxies are in fact moving away from each other. They suggest that perhaps the redshifts are due to something far simpler—such as light losing some of its energy as it crosses billions of miles of space.[28]

If the universe indeed is expanding, young-earth creationists suggest that perhaps God brought the universe into being at some *ongoing stage* in the process of expansion.[29] If I am understanding this suggestion correctly, instead of a "big bang" deriving from a tiny, hot, extremely dense cosmic egg, perhaps God in His mighty power initially "spread out" the galaxies at a great distance from each other, with a continuing ongoing expansion from that distant outer point. If this scenario is correct, it would give the appearance that this expansion has been going on for billions of years when in reality a far shorter time period may be involved (a period more compatible with young-earth creationism).

Young-earth creationists also appeal to the second law of thermodynamics in arguing for the unlikeliness of the big bang scenario (see the appendix). Explosions—especially one as big as the alleged big bang explosion—produce tremendous chaos and disorder, not precise order (as the universe seems to display today). How could a big bang explosion produce "the beauti-fully organized and complexly ordered universe that we now have"?[30]

Another scientific problem with the big bang theory relates to the distribution of matter throughout the universe. If the big bang theory were true, we would expect to see an even and uniform distribution of matter expanding in every direction. Yet this is not what we see. Indeed, our universe has been found to be very clumpy, with various super-clusters of millions of galaxies separated by immense voids in space.[31] Dr. Werner Gitt notes that

> two astronomers, Geller and Huchra, embarked on a measuring program expecting to find evidence to support the big bang model. By compiling large star maps, they hoped to demonstrate that matter is uniformly distributed throughout the cosmos.... The more progress they made with their cartographic overview of space, the clearer it became that distant galaxies are clustered like cosmic continents beyond nearly empty reaches of space. The big bang model was strongly shaken by this discovery.[32]

Yet another scientific problem relates to the background radiation throughout the universe (residual radiation from the big bang). As we just saw, big bang theorists initially postulated that the matter in the universe would be evenly distributed throughout the universe as a result of the cosmic explosion. They also postulated that the level of background radiation in the universe would be smooth. The level of radiation ought to be the same in every direction.

Scientists have indeed discovered that the background radiation is perfectly smooth in every direction. But now *that* finding contradicts the nonuniform distribution of matter throughout the universe. Indeed, as noted above, matter *is not* evenly distributed throughout the universe. Rather, the universe has been found to be very clumpy, with the different clumps separated by huge voids of space. This being the case, young-earth creationists note, there ought to be differences in the level of background radiation, with more radiation in certain directions than in others. But that is not the case.[33]

In view of these and other scientific problems, secular scientists are strongly debating the validity of the big bang theory. Professor Sir Fred Hoyle, one of Britain's greatest astrophysicists, was as strong opponent of the big bang theory and constantly gave it "a good kicking."[34] Among competing theories that have been suggested as replacements for the big bang theory by various scientists are the plasma theory, the steady state theory, the string theory, the multiple-universe theory, and a number of variations of the inflation theory (over 50 variations).[35] Space prohibits examining all these theories, but they all involve untested ideas and a high degree of speculation.[36] Henry Morris reflects, "I try to scan two dozen or more scientific journals each month, and it seems to me there is no end to the speculative writings and researches on these topics."[37]

The fact that much of the scientific community is raising serious problems with the big bang theory should give one pause in accepting it. Debate among scientists on this issue seems more heated than ever.

Even apart from such scientific problems, young-earth creationists point out that the big bang scenario conflicts with Scripture. For example, the big bang theory postulates that the earth formed long after the stars formed, but the Bible says the earth was created *prior* to the stars. Likewise, the big bang theory says the sun formed before the earth did, but the Bible says the sun was created on the fourth day, *after* the earth (see Genesis 1:14-19). Moreover, whereas the big bang theory speaks of stars and planets emerging long, long after the initial cosmic explosion (by hundreds of millions of years), Scripture indicates that God spoke the word and the universe suddenly leaped into existence. Psalm 33:9 says, "For he spoke, and it came to be; he commanded, and it stood firm."

For these (and other) reasons, young-earth creationists generally believe the big bang theory involves a misinterpretation of the observable data—especially in regard to the so-called redshift. And in view of the fact that many prominent secular scientists are giving the theory a big "thumbs down" today, they feel that before long, the big bang will go out with a little whimper.

A Reflection

I close this chapter with two brief observations:

Scientific theories change over time. New discoveries have consistently caused old scientific paradigms to be discarded in favor of newer paradigms. Science historian Thomas Kuhn proved this in his book *The Structure of Scientific Revolutions.* As I write, many scientists are discarding the big bang theory. (On my desk at the moment are a number of articles documenting this, including titles like "Leading Cosmologists Challenge Big Bang Theory," and "Two Prominent Theorists Propose Alternative to Big-Bang Theory," and "No More Big Bang? Stanford U. Research Presents New Beginning to Universe.") Who knows where the discussion will lead? I certainly don't know.

God's Word does not change over time. Jesus asserted that "heaven and earth will pass away, but my words will not pass away" (Mark 13:31). God's Word is a rock-solid foundation you can always trust. The Word of God does not change or falter. It is not a "here today, gone tomorrow" proposition. God's Word is trustworthy *forever*.

Why do I make these observations? I make them because science (a discipline that I *do* have some respect for[38]) may uncover insights to help us better understand the creation described in Genesis. Yet we must not ever make our under-standing of Scripture dependent upon the ever-changing field of science. If you put all your stock in a particular scientific theory (such as the big bang theory) as a support for your bibli-cal position, and then scientists discover irresolvable problems with that scientific theory, what happens to your biblical posi-tion? Will you still hold to it, or will you change it along with the changing scientific paradigm? I personally have a problem with such instability.

Better to place your complete faith in Scripture while still respecting science than to place your complete faith in science while wavering back and forth on Scripture. This modus operandi has the benefit of being open to whatever science correctly and legitimately reveals, while at the same time anchor-ing your beliefs and worldview on the rock that cannot be moved: the Word of God. To me, the Christian really has no choice but to follow this modus operandi, especially in view of the fact that science today rests wholly on the foundation of naturalistic philosophy.

The Second Law of Thermodynamics Argues Against Evolution

The first and second laws of thermodynamics are foundational to science and have never been contradicted in observable nature. This may sound like a topic you'd rather avoid, but these laws have direct application to the validity of evolutionary theory.

The First Law of Thermodynamics

The first law of thermodynamics is the law of energy conservation and says that energy cannot be created nor destroyed—it can only change forms. The total amount of energy remains constant and unchanged. The late atheistic scientist Isaac Asimov said that in over 125 years, scientists have not witnessed a single violation of this fundamental law.[1]

The Second Law of Thermodynamics

The second law of thermodynamics says that in an isolated system (a system that neither loses energy nor gains it from outside of itself, like our universe), the natural course of things is to degenerate. The universe is running down, not evolving upward. Although the total amount of energy remains constant and unchanged, it becomes less available for usable work as time goes on.

Asimov noted that the second law basically means that the universe is getting increasingly disorderly. Clean up a room and it quickly becomes messy again. Clean up a kitchen and watch how fast it becomes disorderly again. "How difficult to maintain houses, and machinery, and our own bodies in perfect working order; how easy to let them deteriorate. In fact, all we have to do is nothing, and everything deteriorates, collapses, breaks down, wears out, all by itself—and that is what the second law is all about."[2]

This second law can be described in terms of "entropy." An increase in entropy involves a transition from a more orderly state to a less orderly state—like a cleaned-up bedroom becoming messy.

Implications of These Laws

Based on the first and second laws of thermodynamics, creationists believe our universe is headed toward an ultimate "heat death" in which no more energy will be converted.[3] The amount of usable energy will eventually deplete. Our universe is decaying. It is eroding.[4] It is moving from order to disorder. The universe—and everything in the universe, including our sun, our bodies, the machines we build, and my car—is running down.

This means that, contrary to evolutionary theory, things are not ultimately moving upward but are rather running downward. The foundational principle of biological evolution—that things are moving from disorder to order, from chaos to complexity—is simply wrong.[5] "The principle of evolution is precisely the converse of the second law of thermodynamics, and therefore both cannot simultaneously be true."[6]

The laws of thermodynamics add strong support for the idea of a creation. If the second law of thermodynamics is true, then the universe must not be eternal. Therefore, the universe must have had a beginning, just as Genesis 1:1 claims. Lincoln Barnett, in his book *The Universe and Dr. Einstein*, writes:

> If the universe is running down and nature's processes are proceeding in just one direction [entropy], the inescapable inference is that everything had a beginning; somehow and sometime the cosmic processes were started, the stellar fires ignited, and the whole vast pageant of the universe brought into being.[7]

If you compare the universe to a clock, there had to be a time when the clock had to be fully wound up.[8] This implies the existence of a Creator who initiated things in the beginning.

John C. Whitcomb, in his book *The Early Earth*, similarly notes that the second law of thermodynamics points us to the reality that planet earth was once more orderly and organized than it is now. And this in turn points to "an infinite and personal God who alone could have infused order and high-level energy into the universe at the beginning."[9]

In keeping with this, J.W.N. Sullivan, in *The Limitations of Science*, points to the fact that the universe absolutely had to have a beginning:

> The fact that the energy of the universe will be more disorganized tomorrow than it is today implies, of course, the fact that the energy of the universe is more highly organized today than it will be tomorrow, and that it was more highly organized yesterday than it is today. Following the process backwards we find a more and more highly organized universe. This backward tracing in time cannot be continued indefinitely. Organization cannot, as it were, mount up and up without limit. There is a definite maximum, and this definite maximum must have been in existence a finite

time ago. And it is impossible that this state of perfect organization could have been evolved from some less perfect state. Nor is it possible that the universe could have persisted for eternity in that state of perfect organization and then suddenly, a finite time ago, have begun to pursue its present path. Thus the accepted laws of nature lead us to a definite beginning of the universe in time.[10]

The "running down" of the universe is well illustrated by the sun. Scientists tell us that our sun is burning off its own mass at a rate of four million tons per second. Since the sun does not regenerate—it does not produce any new mass—the mass that is burning off can never be regained once it is gone. We do not need to be rocket scientists to come to the conclusion that if four million tons of mass are burning away every second, then eventually, given enough time, the sun will simply run out of mass to burn. What is true with our own sun is also true of the millions of stars in the universe. They're all burning away mass at a phenomenal pace. And one day, the universe will experience a "heat death." *Show over!*

But don't forget the main point. If the sun is continually burning off its mass, and its available energy is continually being depleted, then the sun (and all the other stars) must have been created and infused with all this energy at some time.[11] Since our universe is not yet dead, and since it will one day *be* dead (as all the energy runs out), the universe obviously must have had a beginning.

To say the universe is eternal would be nonsensical. After all, all the stars are burning out. If time reached back eternally into the past, our universe would have burned out long ago. What the Bible says makes much more sense—that is, the space-time universe was created at a point in time (see Genesis 1:1; John 1:3; Colossians 1:16).[12]

Biblical Support for These Laws

The Bible provides evidence for the scientific laws we have
been discussing—and the Bible precedes the formulation of these
laws by thousands of years! The Bible is clear that this universe,
and all that is within the universe, is running down. This
includes our human bodies. Noting the brevity of life, Job, the
great Old Testament servant of God, said that "man born of
woman is of few days" (Job 14:1). He appealed to God,
"Remember, O God, that my life is but a breath" (7:7).

The psalmist likewise pondered before God, "You have made
my days a mere handbreadth; the span of my years is as nothing before you. Each man's life is but a breath" (Psalm 39:5).
Reflecting back over his life, he said, "My days vanish like smoke"
(102:3).

The New Testament continues this emphasis on man's
brevity. In James 4:14 we are told, "You do not even know what
will happen tomorrow. What is your life? You are a mist that
appears for a little while and then vanishes." First Peter 1:24
likewise instructs us that "all men are like grass, and all their
glory is like the flowers of the field; the grass withers and the
flowers fall." Life is short. The days relentlessly pass. We grow
old so quickly. And then we die. Entropy rules.

As for the universe, Psalm 102:25-27 speaks of how it will
one day pass away: "In the beginning you laid the foundations
of the earth, and the heavens are the work of your hands. They
will perish, but you remain; they will all wear out like a garment.
Like clothing you will change them and they will be discarded.
But you remain the same, and your years will never end" (see
also Hebrews 1:10-12). The description of the universe perish-
ing and wearing out like an old garment is a graphic illustration of the second law of thermodynamics.

Likewise, in Isaiah 51:6 we read, "Lift up your eyes to the
heavens, look at the earth beneath; the heavens will vanish like
smoke, the earth will wear out like a garment and its inhabitants

die like flies. But my salvation will last forever, my righteousness will never fail." The "heavens" in this verse refers not to the domain of God but rather to earth's atmosphere and interstellar space. Scripture speaks of three heavens. The first heaven is earth's atmosphere (Job 35:5). The second heaven is that of interstellar universe (Genesis 1:17; Deuteronomy 17:3). The third heaven is the ineffable and glorious dwelling place of God in all His glory (2 Corinthians 12:2), elsewhere called the "heaven of heavens" and the "highest heaven" (1 Kings 8:27; 2 Chronicles 2:6). Isaiah 51:6 teaches that the first two heavens—earth's atmosphere and interstellar space—will vanish like smoke.

Jesus likewise taught that "heaven and earth will pass away, but my words will never pass away" (Matthew 24:35; see also Mark 13:31 and Luke 21:33). The apostle Paul addresses the reason *why* heaven and earth will pass away:

> The creation was subjected to frustration, not by its own choice, but by the will of the one who subjected it, in hope that the creation itself will be liberated from its bondage to decay and brought into the glorious freedom of the children of God. We know that the whole creation has been groaning as in the pains of childbirth right up to the present time (Romans 8:20-22).

When did this "bondage to decay" begin? Christians have different views on this, but the great majority believe this bondage began at the fall of man. As a result of man's sin against God, man's entire domain was judged by God. Other Christians believe the universe began winding down as soon as He created it—that is, the stars began burning off their mass as soon as they were created.[13]

The good news is that one day this bondage will end and God will renew the universe. Before we can see the eternal kingdom, God must deal with this cursed earth. Indeed, the earth—along with the first and second heavens (the earth's atmosphere and the stellar universe)—must be renewed. The old must make room for the new.[14]

In the book of Revelation we read, "Then I saw a new heaven and a new earth, for the first heaven and the first earth had passed away, and there was no longer any sea.... He who was seated on the throne said, 'I am making everything new!'" (Revelation 21:1,5). The Greek word used to designate the newness of the cosmos is *kainos*. This word means "new in nature" or "new in quality." Hence, the phrase "new heavens and a new earth" refers not to a cosmos that is totally other than the present cosmos. Rather, the new cosmos will stand in continuity with the present cosmos, but it will be utterly renewed and renovated.[15]

In keeping with this, Matthew 19:28 speaks of "the renewal of all things." Acts 3:21 speaks of the restoration of all things. The new earth, being a renewed and an eternal earth, will be adapted to the vast moral and physical changes that the eternal state necessitates. Everything will be new in the eternal state. Everything will be according to God's own glorious nature. The new heavens and the new earth will be brought into blessed conformity with all that God is in a state of fixed bliss and absolute perfection. No more decay. No more deterioration. No more disorder. While entropy seems to rule now, a day is coming when all things will truly be made new for ever and ever.

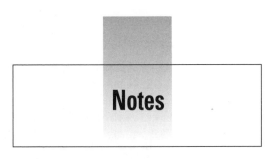

Notes

The Creation vs. Evolution Debate: Why It Matters

1. Robert C. Cowen, "New Evidence Gives Credence to the Big-Bang Theory," *The Christian Science Monitor*, May 14, 2003, online report.

2. "350,000-Year-Old Footprints Discovered," Associated Press, March 13, 2003, online report.

3. "It Was A Dino-Eats-Dino World," Associated Press, April 2, 2003, online report. See also John Roach, "Dinosaur Cannibal: Fossil Evidence Found in Africa," *National Geographic News*, April 2, 2003, online report.

4. Jeremy Lovell, "T-Rex, Merciless Killer or Garbage Disposal Unit?" Reuters News Service, 2003, ABCNEWS online report.

5. Phillip E. Johnson, *Defeating Darwinism by Opening Minds* (Downers Grove, IL: InterVarsity Press, 1997), p. 10. See also William A. Dembski and James M. Kushiner, eds. *Signs of Intelligence* (Grand Rapids, MI: Brazos Press, 2001), p. 27.

6. Johnson, p. 11.

7. See Robert Lightner, *Evangelical Theology: A Survey and Review* (Grand Rapids, MI: Baker Book House, 1986), p. 154.

8. Class notes, "Theology 402," David J. MacLeod, Dallas Theological Seminary, 1980.

9. Del Ratzsch, *The Battle of Beginnings: Why Neither Side Is Winning the Creation-Evolution Debate* (Downers Grove, IL: InterVarsity Press, 1996), p. 19.

10. David J. MacLeod, "Postulates of Lamarck and Darwin," class notes for "Theology 402," Dallas Theological Seminary, 1980.

11. John Hutchison notes that Darwin's "writings show very little personal piety or knowledge of the Scriptures, and whatever theism he held turned to agnosticism after 1860." "Darwin's Evolutionary Theory and 19th-Century Natural Theology," *Bibliotheca Sacra* (Dallas, TX: Dallas Theological Seminary [Electronic edition by Galaxie Software]), 1999.

12. Randal Keynes, *Annie's Box: Charles Darwin, His Daughter, and Human Evolution* (New York: Riverhead Books, 2001), pp. 54-55.

13. Charles Darwin and Nora Barlow, *The Autobiography of Charles Darwin 1809–1882* (New York: W.W. Norton & Company, 1993), pp. 92-93.

14. Keynes, p. 131.

15. Darwin and Barlow, p. 86.

16. Darwin and Barlow, p. 86.

17. Keynes, inside front jacket, insert added.

18. Keynes, p. 243.

19. Michael Denton, *Evolution: A Theory in Crisis* (Chevy Chase, MD: Adler & Adler, 1985), p. 44.

20. *Signs of Intelligence*, p. 45.

21. Hugh Ross, *The Creator and the Cosmos* (Colorado Springs, CO: NavPress, 2001), pp. 13-14.

22. Dylan Evans and Howard Selina, *Introducing Evolution* (Cambridge: Totem Books, 2001), p. 6.

23. Ken Ham, *The Lie* (El Cajon, CA: Master Books, 1991), p. xii.

24. William Provine, cited in *Signs of Intelligence*, p. 45.

25. Henry Morris, *The Biblical Basis for Modern Science* (Grand Rapids, MI: Baker Book House, 1984), pp. 392-93.

26. John C. Whitcomb, *The Early Earth* (Grand Rapids, MI: Baker Books, 1979), p. 111.

27. John C. Whitcomb and Henry M. Morris, *The Genesis Flood: The Biblical Record and Its Scientific Implications* (Grand Rapids, MI: Baker Book House, 1980), p. 21.

28. Huston Smith, "Evolution and Evolutionism," *Christian Century*, July 7-14, 1982, p. 755.

29. Evans and Selina, p. 6.

30. Evans and Selina, p. 6.

31. Richard Dawkins, *Signs of Intelligence*, p. 44.

32. *Humanist Manifesto II,* American Humanist Association, 1973.

33. James Hitchcock, *What Is Secular Humanism?* (Ann Arbor, MI: Servant Books, 1982), Introduction.

34. Isaac Asimov interview by Paul Kurtz, "An Interview with Isaac Asimov on Science and the Bible," *Free Inquiry,* Vol. 2, Spring 1982, p. 9.

35. Carl Sagan, *Cosmos* (New York: Ballantine Books, 1985), p. 1.

36. Isaac Asimov, *Isaac Asimov's Book of Science and Nature Quotations* (New York: Weidenfeld & Nicolson, 1988), p. xvi.

37. Frederick Edwords, "The Humanist Philosophy in Perspective," *The Humanist,* January/February 1984 (n.p.).

38. Cited in *Christianity and Humanism* (n.p., n.d.), 12; on file at Christian Research Institute, Rancho Santa Margarita, CA.

39. *Christianity and Humanism*, p. 12.

40. *Christianity and Humanism*, p. 12.

41. *Humanist Manifesto II.*

42. Paul Kurtz, *Forbidden Fruit: The Ethics of Humanism* (Buffalo, NY: Prometheus Books, 1988), p. 243.

43. *Humanist Manifesto II.*

44. Hank Hanegraaff, *The Face that Demonstrates the Farce of Evolution* (Nashville, TN: W Publishing Group, 1998), p. 28.

45. Peter Hoffman, *Hitler's Personal Security*, 264; cited in Ham, p. 85.

46. Stephen Jay Gould, *I Have Landed: The End of a Beginning in Natural History* (New York: Harmony Books, 2002), p. 336.

47. James W. English, "Could Racism Be Hereditary?," *Eternity*, September 1970, p. 22.

48. Buckner H. Payne, *The Negro: What Is His Ethnological Status?* 2nd ed. (Cincinnati, OH: 1867), pp. 45-46; summarized by Millard J. Erickson, *Christian Theology* (Grand Rapids, MI: Baker Book House, 1983), p. 543.

49. See Hanegraaff, pp. 24-25.

50. See Hanegraaff, p. 29.

51. Duane T. Gish, *Evolution: The Fossils Still Say No!* (El Cajon, CA: Institute for Creation Research, 1995), p. 5.

52. Gish, p. 3. Evolutionists will try to argue that evolution has been observed, but in every case that this claim is made, *microevolution* (that is, evolution *within* a particular species) has been observed, not *macroevolution* (evolution of one species into another).

53. Phillip E. Johnson, *Reason in the Balance: The Case Against Naturalism in Science, Law and Education* (Downers Grove, IL: InterVarsity Press, 1995), p. 21, insert added.

54. Norman Geisler and Joseph Holden, *Living Loud: Defending Your Faith* (Nashville, TN: Broadman & Holman Publishers, 2002), p. 64.

55. See Johnson, *Defeating Darwinism by Opening Minds*, pp. 41-42. Evolutionists may *claim* there are intermediate fossils. They may *claim* to have evidence for positive mutations. I evaluate these claims later in the book.

56. Evans and Selina, p. 22.

57. Ross, p. 163.

58. Johnson, *Defeating Darwinism by Opening Minds*, p. 35.

59. Richard Dawkins, "Put Your Money on Evolution," *The New York Times Review of Books*, April 9, 1989, p. 35.

Chapter 1—There Are Different Kinds of Evolution

1. *Evolution: A Handbook for Students by a Medical Scientist* (Toronto: International Christian Crusade, 1951), p. 7.

2. See Chris Colby, "Evolution," *The World and I*, Vol. 11, January 1, 1996, 294, Electric Library.

3. Dylan Evans and Howard Selina, *Introducing Evolution* (Cambridge: Totem Books, 2001), p. 8.

4. J. William Schopf, *Evolution: Facts and Fallacies* (San Diego, CA: Academic Press, 1999), p. 146.

5. Michael Benton, "Introduction: Life and Time," in *The Book of Life*, ed. Stephen Jay Gould (New York: W.W. Norton & Company, 2001), p. 29.

6. Millard Erickson, *Christian Theology* (Grand Rapids, MI: Baker Book House, 1985), p. 479.

7. Jonathan Wells, "Issues in the Creation-Evolution Controversies," *The World and I*, Vol. 11, January 1, 1996, p. 294, Electric Library.

8. Ernst Mayr, *What Evolution Is* (New York: Basic Books, 2001), p. 288.

9. Mayr, p. 118.

10. See "Natural Selection," *The Hutchinson Dictionary of Science*, January 1, 1998, Electric Library.

11. Evans and Selina, p. 34.

12. *The Science of Biology* (New York: McGraw-Hill, 1963), p. 39.

13. Ralph O. Muncaster, *Dismantling Evolution* (Eugene, OR: Harvest House Publishers, 2003), p. 14.

14. Colby, "Evolution," Electric Library.

15. Evans and Selina, p. 11.

16. Schopf, p. 17. See also Richard Fortey, *Life: A Natural History of the First Four Billion Years of Life on Earth* (New York: Alfred A. Knopf, 1997), p. 240. See also Benton, p. 25.

17. "Uniformitarianism," *The Hutchinson Dictionary of Science*. See also Ken Ham, *The Lie* (El Cajon, CA: Master Books, 1991), pp. 123-24.

18. Ham, p. 124.

19. John C. Whitcomb and Henry M. Morris, *The Genesis Flood: The Biblical Record and Its Scientific Implications* (Grand Rapids, MI: Baker Book House, 1980), p. xvi.

20. Benton, p. 29.

21. Some intelligent Christians believe in a young earth, and some intelligent Christians believe in an old earth. While Christians may have disagreements on this issue, they agree that microevolution does not constitute proof for macroevolution. Of course, Christians who believe in theistic evolution are in a category all their own, and I discuss their position later in the book.

22. Wells, "Issues in the Creation-Evolution Controversies," Electric Library.

23. Del Ratzsch, *The Battle of Beginnings: Why Neither Side Is Winning the Creation-Evolution Debate* (Downers Grove, IL: InterVarsity Press, 1996), p. 49.

24. Evolutionist Ernst Mayr describes *microevolution* as "evolution at or below the species level," and *macroevolution* as "evolution above the species level; the evolution of higher taxa and the production of evolutionary novelties, such as new structures." *What Evolution Is*, pp. 286-87.

25. William Nowers, "Darwinism in Denial," *The Washington Times*, November 25, 2001, Electric Library.

26. Johnson, p. 87.

27. Hank Hanegraaff, *The Face that Demonstrates the Farce of Evolution* (Nashville, TN: W Publishing Group, 1998), p. 172.

28. Colby, "Evolution," Electric Library.

29. David H. Lane, "Special Creation or Evolution: No Middle Ground," *Bibliotheca Sacra* (Dallas, TX: Dallas Theological Seminary [Electronic edition by Galaxie Software]) 1999. See also Muncaster, pp. 67-68.

30. See Steve Jones, *Darwin's Ghost: The Origin of Species Updated* (New York: Random House, 2000), pp. 69-101.

31. *The American Heritage Dictionary of the English Language*, Fourth Edition (Houghton Mifflin Company, 2000), electronic online edition.

32. See Phillip E. Johnson, *Darwin on Trial* (Downers Grove, IL: InterVarsity Press, 1993), p. 69.

33. Wells, "Issues in the Creation-Evolution Controversies," Electric Library.

34. Rachel D. Ramer, "In Debate with Evolutionists," Statement DC742, Christian Research Institute, Rancho Santa Margarita, CA.

35. Phillip E. Johnson, *Defeating Darwinism by Opening Minds* (Downers Grove, IL: InterVarsity Press, 1997), p. 58.

36. Norman Geisler and Joseph Holden, *Living Loud: Defending Your Faith* (Nashville, TN: Broadman & Holman Publishers, 2002), p. 57.

37. As noted by Ratzsch, p. 30.

38. Ratzsch, pp. 33-34.

39. Julian Huxley, "Evolution and Genetics," in *What Is Science?* ed. J.R. Newman (New York: Simon and Schuster, 1955), p. 272.

Chapter 2—Evolutionism Rests on the Foundation of Naturalism

1. See "Naturalism," *The Columbia Encyclopedia*, 7th ed., January 1, 2002, online edition.

2. See, for example, *Signs of Intelligence*, eds. William A. Dembski and James M. Kushiner (Grand Rapids, MI: Brazos Press, 2001), p. 46.

3. Del Ratzsch, *The Battle of Beginnings: Why Neither Side Is Winning the Creation-Evolution Debate* (Downers Grove, IL: InterVarsity Press, 1996), p. 14.

4. William A. Dembski, *Intelligent Design: The Bridge Between Science & Theology* (Downers Grove, IL: InterVarsity Press, 1999), p. 103. See also Michael J. Behe, "Huxley: From Devil's Disciple to Evolution's High Priest," Book Reviews, *National Review*, Vol. 50, February 9, 1998, p. 54.

5. Dembski, *Intelligent Design: The Bridge Between Science & Theology*, p. 103.

6. Phillip E. Johnson, *Reason in the Balance: The Case Against Naturalism in Science, Law and Education* (Downers Grove, IL: InterVarsity Press, 1995), p. 38.

7. See Phillip E. Johnson, *Defeating Darwinism by Opening Minds* (Downers Grove, IL: InterVarsity Press, 1997), p. 21.

8. Paul Kurtz, "Symposium on Humanist Manifesto II: Beyond Humanist Manifesto II," *The Humanist*, Vol. 58, September 19, 1998, online edition.

9. Julian Huxley, Associated Press Dispatch, November 27, 1959, Address at Darwin Centennial Convocation, Chicago University, see *Issues in Evolution*, ed. Sol Tax (Chicago, IL: University of Chicago Press, 1960).

10. See Johnson, *Reason in the Balance*, p. 75.

11. "To introduce occult or transcendental causes is inadmissible within the sciences." Kurtz, "Symposium on Humanist Manifesto II: Beyond Humanist Manifesto II."

12. Behe, "Huxley: From Devil's Disciple to Evolution's High Priest," *National Review*, p. 54.

13. See Dembski, *Intelligent Design: The Bridge Between Science & Theology*, p. 100.

14. Behe, "Huxley: From Devil's Disciple to Evolution's High Priest," *National Review*, p. 54.

15. Michael J. Behe, *Darwin's Black Box* (New York: The Free Press, 1996), pp. 235-36, insert added.

16. Quoted in Jodie Berndt, *Celebration of Miracles* (Nashville, TN: Thomas Nelson, Inc., 1995), p. 20.

17. Norman L. Geisler, "Miracles, Arguments Against," in *Baker Encyclopedia of Christian Apologetics* (Grand Rapids, MI: Baker Book House, 1999), pp. 457-68.

18. "Religious Doctrines and Dogmas: In the 18th and Early 19th Centuries," *Encyclopedia Britannica*, electronic media.

19. David Hume, *An Enquiry Concerning Human Understanding* (1777), entire essay reproduced in R. Douglas Geivett and Gary R. Habermas, *In Defense of Miracles: A Comprehensive Case for God's Action in History* (Downers Grove, IL: InterVarsity Press, 1997), p. 33.

20. Randal Keynes, *Annie's Box: Charles Darwin, His Daughter, and Human Evolution* (New York: Riverhead Books, 2001), pp. 42-43.

21. Ernst Mayr, *What Evolution Is* (New York: Basic Books, 2001), p. 9.

22. See Mayr, p. 9.

23. Since I do not have the luxury of devoting such space to debunking naturalism, I recommend Phillip Johnson's *Reason in the Balance: The Case Against Naturalism in Science, Law and Education*. See also Ron Rhodes, *Miracles Around Us* (Eugene, OR: Harvest House Publishers, 2000).

24. Johnson, *Defeating Darwinism by Opening Minds*, pp. 92, 114-15.

25. John A. Witmer, "The Doctrine of Miracles," *Bibliotheca Sacra*, Logos Bible Software, electronic media.

26. Louis Berkhof, *Systematic Theology* (Grand Rapids, MI: Eerdmans, 1982), p. 177.

27. Charles Ryrie, *Survey of Bible Doctrine*, QuickVerse Library, electronic media.

28. Berkhof, p. 177.

29. Quoted in Norman L. Geisler and Ronald M. Brooks, *When Skeptics Ask* (Wheaton, IL: Victor Press, 1989), p. 76.

30. Geisler and Brooks, p. 76.

31. Ken Boa and Larry Moody, *I'm Glad You Asked* (Wheaton, IL: Victor Books, 1994), pp. 50-51.

32. Boa and Moody, p. 53.

33. Peter Kreeft and Ronald Tacelli, *Handbook of Christian Apologetics* (Downers Grove, IL: InterVarsity Press, 1994), p. 109.

34. David Hume, *An Enquiry Concerning Human Understanding* (1777), in Geivett and Habermas, p. 33.

35. Norman Geisler, "Miracles and the Modern Mind," chapter 4, Geivett and Habermas, p. 78. See also Henry Clarence Thiessen, *Lectures in Systematic Theology* (Grand Rapids, MI: Eerdmans, 1979), p. 12.

36. Geisler and Brooks, pp. 79-80.

37. Paul E. Little, *Know Why You Believe* (Downers Grove, IL: InterVarsity Press, 1975), p. 59.

38. Charles Hodge, *Systematic Theology*, Logos Bible Software, electronic media, insert added.

39. Geisler, *Baker Encyclopedia of Christian Apologetics*, p. 450.

40. Isaac Asimov admitted he could not prove that God did not exist. Isaac Asimov interview by Paul Kurtz, "An Interview with Isaac Asimov on Science and the Bible," *Free Inquiry*, Vol. 2, Spring 1982, p. 9.

41. J.P. Moreland, ed., *The Creation Hypothesis: Scientific Evidence for an Intelligent Designer* (Downers Grove, IL: InterVarsity Press, 1994), p. 116.

Chapter 3—Christians Have Diverse Views

1. See William R. Wineke, "Much Gray Area in Debate on World's Birth," *Wisconsin State Journal*, February 2, 1997, p. 10A, online edition.

2. Gordon R. Lewis and Bruce A. Demarest, *Integrative Theology* (Grand Rapids, MI: Zondervan, 1996), II:23.

3. See A.F. Johnson, "Gap Theory," *The Concise Evangelical Dictionary of Theology*, ed. Walter A. Elwell (Grand Rapids, MI: Baker Book House, 1991), p. 192.

4. Millard Erickson, *Christian Theology* (Grand Rapids, MI: Baker Book House, 1985), p. 380.

5. Charles Ryrie, *Basic Theology* (Wheaton, IL: Victor Books, 1986), p. 183.

6. Donald Grey Barnhouse, *The Invisible War* (Grand Rapids, MI: Zondervan, 1965), p. 9.

7. Barnhouse, p. 19.

8. Barnhouse, p. 61.

9. Barnhouse, p. 22.

10. Henry Morris, *The Biblical Basis for Modern Science* (Grand Rapids, MI: Baker Book House, 1984), p. 121.

11. H.L. Willmington, *Willmington's Guide to the Bible* (Wheaton, IL: Tyndale House Publishers, 1984), p. 19.

12. John C. Whitcomb, *The Early Earth* (Grand Rapids, MI: Baker Book House, 1979), p. 116.

13. Vern S. Poythress, "Response to Robert C. Newman," *Three Views on Creation and Evolution*, eds. J.P. Moreland and John Mark Reynolds (Grand Rapids, MI: Zondervan, 1999), p. 149.

14. Erickson, p. 384.

15. Loren Haarsma, "Why Believe in a Creator?: Perspectives on Evolution," *The World and I*, Vol. 11, January 1, 1996, p. 322, online edition.

16. See P.P.T. Pun, "Evolution," in *Evangelical Dictionary of Theology*, ed. Walter A. Elwell (Grand Rapids, MI: Baker Book House, 1984), p. 389.

17. Erickson, p. 384.

18. Robert C. Newman, "Progressive Creationism," *Three Views on Creation and Evolution*, p. 106.

19. Gleason L. Archer, *Encyclopedia of Bible Difficulties* (Grand Rapids, MI: Zonderan, 1982), p. 60.

20. See Pun, p. 389.

21. Lewis and Demarest, II:29.

22. Newman, "Progressive Creationism," p. 107.

23. Hugh Ross, *The Creator and the Cosmos* (Colorado Springs, CO: NavPress, 2001), p. 78.

24. Norman Geisler and Thomas Howe, *When Critics Ask: A Popular Handbook on Bible Difficulties*, The Norman Geisler CD-ROM Library (Grand Rapids, MI: Baker Book House), 2002.

25. Pun, p. 392.

26. Haarsma, "Why Believe in a Creator?: Perspectives on Evolution."

27. Morris, *The Biblical Basis for Modern Science*, p. 117.

28. Ryrie, *Basic Theology*, p. 185.

29. Don Batten, ed., *The Revised and Expanded Answers Book* (Green Forest, AR: Master Books, 1990), pp. 37-38.

30. W.E. Vine, Merrill F. Unger, William White, eds. *Vine's Expository Dictionary of Biblical Words* (Nashville, TN: Thomas Nelson, Inc., 1995), p. 72.

31. Whitcomb, 28. See also Ryrie, p. 186.

32. Morris, *The Biblical Basis for Modern Science*, pp. 128-29.

33. *The Revised and Expanded Answers Book*, pp. 46-47.

34. *The Revised and Expanded Answers Book*, p. 48.

35. Whitcomb, 27-28. See also *The Revised and Expanded Answers Book*, p. 44.

36. Robert Lightner, *Evangelical Theology: A Survey and Review* (Grand Rapids, MI: Baker Book House, 1986), p. 178.

37. See Ron Rhodes, *The Complete Book of Bible Answers* (Eugene, OR: Harvest House Publishers, 1997), p. 155.

38. David H. Lane, "Special Creation or Evolution: No Middle Ground," *Bibliotheca Sacra* (Dallas, TX: Dallas Theological Seminary [Electronic edition by Galaxie Software]) 1999.

39. Haarsma, "Why Believe in a Creator?: Perspectives on Evolution."

40. Haarsma, "Why Believe in a Creator?: Perspectives on Evolution."

41. Quoted in Charles Ryrie, *You Mean the Bible Teaches That?* (Chicago, IL: Moody Press, 1976), p. 108.

42. Lane, "Theological Problems with Theistic Evolution."

43. "Teaching Notes for 'A is for Adam'," Answers in Genesis, copyright 1996–1999, at www.christiananswers.net.

44. See Paul Nelson and John Mark Reynolds, "Young Earth Creationism," *Three Views on Creation and Evolution*, p. 56.

45. Whitcomb, p. 104.

46. Lane, "Theological Problems with Theistic Evolution."

47. Haarsma, "Why Believe in a Creator?: Perspectives on Evolution." See also Bryn Nelson, "Six Days of Creation," *Newsday*, March 11, 2002, p. D06, online edition.

48. The following summary is drawn from Morris, *The Biblical Basis for Modern Science*; Henry M. Morris, *Scientific Creationism* (Green Forest, AR: Master Books, 2001); and Whitcomb.

49. Erickson, p. 383.

50. Duane T. Gish, *Evolution: The Fossils Still Say No!* (El Cajon, CA: Institute for Creation Research, 1995), p. 34.

51. Paul Nelson and John Mark Reynolds, "Conclusion," *Three Views on Creation and Evolution*, p. 97.

52. See Douglas Belkin, "God vs. Darwin—Faith vs. Science—Adam vs. an Ape," *The Palm Beach Post*, August 22, 1999, p. 1D, online edition.

53. See Whitcomb, p. 30.

54. Del Ratzsch, *The Battle of Beginnings: Why Neither Side Is Winning the Creation-Evolution Debate* (Downers Grove, IL: InterVarsity Press, 1996), pp. 70-71.

55. Ron Rhodes, *What Did Jesus Mean? Making Sense of the Difficult Sayings of Jesus* (Eugene, OR: Harvest House Publishers, 1999), pp. 155-56.

56. Ron Rhodes, *Miracles Around Us: How to Recognize God at Work Today* (Eugene, OR: Harvest House Publishers, 2000), p. 99.

57. Whitcomb, p. 30.

58. Ratzsch, pp. 70-71.

59. John C. Whitcomb and Henry M. Morris, *The Genesis Flood: The Biblical Record and Its Scientific Implications* (Grand Rapids, MI: Baker Book House, 1980), p. 369.

60. Ratzsch, p. 97.

61. See Stephen Jay Gould, ed., *The Book of Life* (New York: W.W. Norton, 2001), pp. 33-34, 46-48, 227, 251.

62. Richard Fortey, *Life: A Natural History of the First Four Billion Years of Life on Earth* (New York: Alfred A. Knopf, 1997), p. 240; J. William Schopf, *Evolution: Facts and Fallacies* (San Diego, CA: Academic Press, 1999), p. 17.

63. Ratzsch, p. 97.

64. Henry M. Morris, "Biblical Catastrophism and Modern Science," *Bibliotheca Sacra* (Dallas, TX: Dallas Theological Seminary [Electronic edition by Galaxie Software]) 1999. See also Morris, *Scientific Creationism*, p. 97.

65. Morris, *The Biblical Basis for Modern Science*, p. 350.

66. Douglas Belkin, "God vs. Darwin—Faith vs. Science—Adam vs. an Ape," *The Palm Beach Post*, August 22, 1999, p. 1D, online edition.

Chapter 4—The Fossils Argue Against Evolution

1. As noted by Phillip E. Johnson, *Defeating Darwinism by Opening Minds* (Downers Grove, IL: InterVarsity Press, 1997), p. 62.

2. *Webster's Revised Unabridged Dictionary* (Micra, Inc., 1998), Internet edition.

3. WordNet 1.6 (Princeton University, 1997), Internet edition.

4. *The American Heritage Dictionary of the English Language*, Fourth edition (Houghton Mifflin Company, 2000), Internet edition.

5. See Michael Benton, "Life's Patterns and the Fossil Record," in Stephen Jay Gould, ed., *The Book of Life: An Illustrated History of the Evolution of Life on Earth* (New York: W.W. Norton, 2001), p. 33.

6. Henry Morris, *The Biblical Basis for Modern Science* (Grand Rapids, MI: Baker Book House, 1984), p. 344.

7. H.L. Willmington, *Willmington's Guide to the Bible* (Wheaton, IL: Tyndale House Publishers, 1984), p. 28.

8. Duane T. Gish, *Evolution: The Fossils Still Say No!* (El Cajon, CA: Institute for Creation Research, 1995), p. 27.

9. Michael Denton, *Evolution: A Theory in Crisis* (Chevy Chase, MD: Adler & Adler, 1986), p. 160.

10. Charles Darwin, *On the Origin of Species* (New York: The Modern Library, 1856 reprint), 307; http://www.literaturepage.com/read/darwin-origin-of-species.html.

11. See Ralph O. Muncaster, *Dismantling Evolution* (Eugene, OR: Harvest House Publishers, 2003), pp. 69-73.

12. *The Book of Life*, 1.

13. Richard Dawkins, *The Blind Watchmaker: Why the Evidence of Evolution Reveals a Universe Without Design* (New York: W.W. Norton, 1996), p. 229.

14. I realize some evolutionists believe that certain fossil discoveries, such as that of the archaeopteryx, represent a transitional form. But this is not a legitimate transitional form, as I demonstrate later in the chapter.

15. Named after Cambria, Wales, where massive fossil beds were discovered and studied in the 1800s.

16. See J. William Schopf, *Evolution: Facts and Fallacies* (San Diego, CA: Academic Press, 1999), p. 7; *The Book of Life*, p. 2.

17. Stephen Jay Gould, *I Have Landed: The End of a Beginning in Natural History* (New York: Harmony Books, 2002), p. 251. See also Richard Fortey, *Life: A Natural History of the First Four Billion Years of Life on Earth* (New York: Alfred A. Knopf, 1999), pp. 100-06.

18. William A. Dembski and James M. Kushiner, eds., *Signs of Intelligence* (Grand Rapids, MI: Brazos Press, 2001), p. 149.

19. Dawkins, p. 229.

20. See Phillip E. Johnson, *Darwin on Trial* (Downers Grove, IL: InterVarsity Press, 1993), p. 54.

21. Dawkins, p. 229.

22. Johnson, *Darwin on Trial*, p. 24.

23. Ernst Mayr, *What Evolution Is* (New York: Basic Books, 2001), p. 60.

24. Mayr, p. 59.

25. Steve Jones, *Darwin's Ghost: The Origin of Species Updated* (New York: Random House, 2000), p. 207.

26. *Time* magazine reports that among the Burgess Shale fossils, "Preserved were not just the hard-shelled creatures familiar to Darwin and his contemporaries but also the fossilized remains of soft-bodied beasts like Aysheaia and Ottoia" (J. Madeleine Nash, "When Life Exploded for Billions of Years, Simple Creatures Like Plankton, Bacteria and Algae Ruled the Earth. Then, Suddenly, Life Got Very Complicated," *Time*, December 4, 1995, 66ff.). Bryn Nelson reports that "scientists have discovered some flattened soft-tissue fossils in late Precambrian and Cambrian phosphate-rich layers in Greenland and China" (Bryn Nelson, "Find May Give Clue to Cambrian 'Explosion,'" *Newsday*, July 20, 2001, p. A28).

27. See Henry Morris, *The Biblical Basis for Modern Science* (Grand Rapids, MI: Baker Book House, 1984), p. 339.

28. Over a five- to ten-million year period, which, according to geologists, is a mere geologic eye blink. See Michael J. Behe, *Darwin's Black Box: The Biochemical Challenge to Evolution* (New York: The Free Press, 1996), p. 27; Charles Kingsley Levy, *Evolutionary Wars: A Three-Billion-Year Arms Race* (New York: W.H. Freeman and Company, 1999), pp. 13-14.

29. Phillip Johnson has noted that one museum he is aware of provides "imaginary common ancestors" for various animal groups, which serve to convince the ignorant that transitional links have been discovered. This is nothing more than a deception. See Johnson, *Defeating Darwinism by Opening Minds*, p. 38.

30. Hank Hanegraaff, "FACE the Facts About Evolution," Statement DF803, Christian Research Institute.

31. Stephen Jay Gould, "The Return of Hopeful Monsters," *Natural History* 76 (June-July 1977), p. 24.

32. Stephen Jay Gould, "Evolution's Erratic Pace," *Natural History* 86 (May 1977), pp. 14-15.

33. Stephen Jay Gould, "Is a New and General Theory of Evolution Emerging?" *Paleobiology* 6 (1980), p. 40.

34. Darwin, 160; http://www.literaturepage.com/read/darwin-origin-of-species.html.

35. See Mayr, p. 65; Gould, *I Have Landed*, p. 325; Jones, p. 206; Levy, p. 174; *The Book of Life*, p. 144. Evolutionists also claim that some of the ape-men discoveries also represent transitional forms. See, for example, Rod Caird, *Ape Man: The Story of Human Evolution* (New York: MacMillan, 1994); and Paul Jordan, *Neanderthal: Neanderthal Man and the Story of Human Origins* (Great Britain: Sutton, 1999). I discuss this in a later chapter.

36. See Fortey, p. 47.

37. Morris, *The Biblical Basis for Modern Science*, p. 341.

38. John Noble Wilford, "An Early Bird Mars Theory on Dinosaurs," in Nicholas Wade, ed., *The Science Times Book of Fossils and Evolution* (New York: The Lyons Press, 1998), pp. 65-66. See also "A New Flap Over Birds' Evolutionary Path," *Newsday*, November 19, 1996; Dinshaw K. Dadachanjim, "Origins of Life Reconsidered," *The World and I*, September 1, 1997; James Vicini, "Bird's Descent from Dinosaurs In Doubt," Reuters, November 14, 1996.

39. *The Book of Life*, pp. 29, 32.

40. Dawkins, p. 229.

41. Mayr, p. 289.

42. Gish, pp. 354-55.

43. See *The Book of Life*, p. 32.

44. This summary is based on Muncaster, p. 86.

45. Gish, p. 34.

46. Denton, back flap.

Chapter 5—"Ape-Men" Discoveries Do Not Prove Evolution

1. Del Ratzsch, *The Battle of Beginnings: Why Neither Side Is Winning the Creation-Evolution Debate* (Downers Grove, IL: InterVarsity Press, 1996), p. 42; see also Dylan Evans and Howard Selina, *Introducing Evolution* (Cambridge: Totem Books, 2001), p. 20.

2. Ernst Mayr, *What Evolution Is* (New York: Basic Books, 2001), p. 237. See also Richard Fortey, *Life: A Natural History of the First Four Billion Years of Life on Earth* (New York: Alfred A. Knopf, 1997), p. 291.

3. See Stephen Jay Gould, ed., *The Book of Life* (New York: W.W. Norton & Company, 2001), p. 220.

4. Mayr, p. 235.

5. Mayr, pp. 235-36.

6. Marvin L. Lubenow, *Bones of Contention: A Creationist Assessment of Human Fossils* (Grand Rapids, MI: Baker Book House, 1992), pp. 37-38.

7. See Evans and Selina, p. 140.

8. Dr. William L. Straus, of Johns Hopkins Medical College, and Dr. A.J.E. Cave, of St. Bartholomew's Hospital Medical College in London, published their new findings in 1957. See Richard Milton, *Shattering the Myths of Darwinism* (Rochester, VT: Park Street Press, 1997), p. 202.

9. It is also possible that Neanderthal man had a severe case of arthritis.

10. John D. Morris, "Is Neanderthal in Our Family Tree?" *Back to Genesis*, No. 105b, September 1997, Institute for Creation Research.

11. See Charles Kingsley Levy, *Evolutionary Wars: A Three-Billion-Year Arms Race* (New York: W.H. Freeman and Company, 1999), p. 255. See also Fortey, p. 394; *The Book of Life*, p. 245. Some have suggested the possibility that the thick bones, large heads, ridged eyebrows, and heavy muscles of Neanderthal man may be due to a chronic iodine deficiency and cretinism, though this theory has been much disputed. See Guy Gugliotta, "The Neanderthal: A Modern Man with Disease?" *The Washington Post*, May 24, 1999, Electric Library.

12. See Dave Phillips, "Neanderthals Are Still Human!" *Impact*, No. 323, May 2000, Institute for Creation Research.

13. See Paul Jordan, *Neanderthal: Neanderthal Man and the Story of Human Origins* (Great Britain: Sutton Publishing, 1999), p. 75.

14. Lubenow, pp. 37-38.

15. Jordan, p. 51.

16. *The Book of Life*, p. 245.

17. Jordan, 100. See also Morris, "Is Neanderthal in our Family Tree?"

18. *The Book of Life*, p. 247.

19. Milton, 202. See also Morris, *Scientific Creationism*, pp. 175-76; Gleason L. Archer, *Encyclopedia of Bible Difficulties* (Grand Rapids, MI: Zonderan, 1982), p. 63.

20. Evolutionist John Noble Wilford notes: "New fossil evidence shows that the enigmatic Neanderthals, the last competitors to modern humans in their ascent to global dominion, were still living in Croatia as recently as 33,000 years ago and in southern Spain only 30,000 years ago" (John Noble Wilford, "Neanderthals and Modern Humans Co-Existed Longer Than Thought," Nicholas Wade, ed., *The Science Times Book of Fossils and Evolution* [New York: The Lyons Press, 1998], p. 225). This certainly does not set well with the traditional evolutionary model with a linear development of one species into another (see Phillip E. Johnson, *Defeating Darwinism by Opening Minds* [Downers Grove, IL: InterVarsity Press, 1997], p. 61). Scholars have noted the possibility of the Neanderthals and modern humans interbreeding. If they could, Johnson argues, they should *all* be categorized together as a single species, *Homo sapiens* (61). Some, however, have disputed that interbreeding took place (Paul Recer, "Neanderthals, Humans May Have Never Mixed," AP Online, March 6, 2003).

21. See J. William Schopf, *Evolution: Facts and Fallacies* (San Diego, CA: Academic Press, 1999), p. 39.

22. James Perloff, "Time Magazine's New Age-Man," *Creation Matters*, Vol. 6, No. 4, July/August 2001, p. 2.

23. Fortey, p. 292.

24. See Milton, p. 197.

25. Rudolph Virchow, cited in Perloff, p. 2.

26. Milton, p. 198.

27. See H.L. Willmington, *Willmington's Guide to the Bible* (Wheaton, IL: Tyndale House Publishers, 1984), p. 21.

28. Milton, p. 261.

29. Rod Caird, *Ape-Man: The Story of Human Evolution* (New York: MacMillan, 1994), 68. See also Fortey, p. 291.

30. Caird, p. 69.

31. See Milton, p. 261.

32. Lubenow, p. 42.

33. Caird, p. 71.

34. Caird, p. 71. Various suggestions have been made, however. Possible culprits have included Charles Dawson, Sir Arthur Smith Woodward, Sir Arthur Conan Doyle, Teilhard de Chardin, and Martin Hinton. See Meir Ronnen, "Bones of Contention," *Jerusalem Post*, April 24, 1997, Electric Library; and Jennifer Olson, "Bones in Box Show Culprit Behind Piltdown Fraud," Reuters, May 22, 1996, Electric Library.

35. Perloff, p. 2.

36. Willmington, p. 21.

37. Hank Hanegraaff, *The Face that Demonstrates the Farce of Evolution* (Nashville, TN: W Publishing Group, 1998), pp. 56-57.

38. Hanegraaff, pp. 49-50.

39. Norman Geisler and Joseph Holden, *Living Loud: Defending Your Faith* (Nashville, TN: Broadman & Holman Publishers, 2002), p. 60. Hanegraaff, pp. 49-50.

40. Milton, p. 205; Willmington, p. 22.

41. Mark Ridley, ed., *Evolution* (Oxford: Oxford University Press, 1997), p. 335. See also Fortey, p. 297.

42. John D. Morris, "Was Lucy an Ape-Man?" *Back to Genesis,* No. 11b, November 1989, Institute for Creation Research.

43. *The Book of Life,* p. 236.

44. *The Book of Life,* p. 236.

45. Milton, 206.

46. Morris, "Was Lucy an Ape-Man?"

47. Zuckerman and Oxnard are cited in Perloff, p. 3.

48. Fortey, p. 300.

49. Henry Morris, *The Biblical Basis for Modern Science* (Grand Rapids, MI: Baker Book House, 1984), p. 393.

50. I should note that young-earth and old-earth creationists understand things a bit differently. Young-earth creationists believe that apes have always been apes and humans have always been humans, and that the first true humans were Adam and Eve. No humans or prehuman anthropoids lived before Adam and Eve. Old-earth creationists, by contrast, allow for the possibility of pre-Adamic races of anthropoids who had significant intelligence and resourcefulness but who died out before Adam and Eve came on the scene. Old-earth creationists believe that many of the fossil discoveries relate to living beings who died before the time of Adam and Eve. Related to this, Gleason Archer observes: "There may have been advanced and intelligent hominids who lived and died before Adam, but they were not created in the image of God…. Though these early cave dwellers may have developed certain skills in their pursuit of nourishment and engaged in war with one another—as other animals do—nevertheless there is no archaeological evidence of a true human soul as having animated their bodies." See Archer, pp. 64-65.

51. Milton, p. 199.

52. Milton, p. 199.

53. Steve Jones, *Darwin's Ghost: The Origin of Species Updated* (New York: Random House, 2000), p. 323.

54. Michael D. Lemonick, "How Man Began," *Time,* March 14, 1994, Electric Library.

Chapter 6—Mutations and Natural Selection Cannot Bring About New Species

1. Charles Ryrie, *A Survey of Bible Doctrine* (Chicago, IL: Moody Press), electronic version.

2 *The American Heritage Dictionary of the English Language,* Fourth Edition (Houghton Mifflin Company, 2000), online edition.

3. Ernst Mayr, *What Evolution Is* (New York: Basic Books, 2001), p. 96; Dylan Evans and Howard Selina, *Introducing Evolution* (Cambridge: Totem Books, 2001), p. 55.

4. Lane P. Lester, "Genetics: Enemy of Evolution," *Creation Research Society Quarterly,* Vol. 31 No. 4, 1995, online edition.

5. Lester, "Genetics: Enemy of Evolution."

6. Richard Milton, *Shattering the Myths of Darwinism* (Rochester, VT: Park Street Press, 1997), p. 156.

7. Michael J. Behe, *Darwin's Black Box: The Biochemical Challenge to Evolution* (New York: The Free Press, 1996), p. 41.

8. Mayr, 288. See also Del Ratzsch, *The Battle of Beginnings: Why Neither Side Is Winning the Creation-Evolution Debate* (Downers Grove, IL: InterVarsity Press, 1996), p. 27; Phillip E. Johnson, *Darwin*

on Trial (Downers Grove, IL: InterVarsity Press, 1993), p. 17. Some have noted that survival itself is measured by the number of offspring left behind. See Milton, p. 123.

9. Rod Caird, *Ape-Man: The Story of Human Evolution* (New York: MacMillan, 1994), p. 112.

10. Michael Benton, "Introduction: Life and Time," in Stephen Jay Gould, ed., *The Book of Life* (New York: W.W. Norton & Company, 2001), p. 29.

11. Mayr, 98. See also *The American Heritage Dictionary of the English Language*, online edition; Phillip E. Johnson, *Defeating Darwinism by Opening Minds* (Downers Grove, IL: InterVarsity Press, 1997), p. 58.

12. Jonathan Wells, "Issues in the Creation-Evolution Controversies," *The World and I*, Vol. 11, January 1, 1996, p. 294, Electric Library. See also William A. Dembski and James M. Kushiner, eds., *Signs of Intelligence* (Grand Rapids, MI: Brazos Press, 2001), p. 91; Jimmy H. Davis and Harry L. Poe, *Designer Universe: Intelligent Design and the Existence of God* (Nashville, TN: Broadman & Holman Publishers, 2002), pp. 70-71.

13. Millard Erickson, *Christian Theology* (Grand Rapids, MI: Baker Book House, 1985), p. 479.

14. See Ratzsch, p. 38.

15. Steve Jones, *Darwin's Ghost: The Origin of Species Updated* (New York: Random House, 2000), p. 72. See also Evans and Selina, p. 47. Note, however, that not all agree that this is an example of natural selection at work. Milton writes: "Far from being an example of evolution or even of natural selection, the peppered moth is an example of a shift in population. The same thing would happen in human terms if some disease were to kill off the white race but left the black race unharmed. Similar shifts in balance continually occur among animal and plant populations, where one variety flourishes at the expense of another" (Milton, p. 131).

16. See Ralph O. Muncaster, *Dismantling Evolution* (Harvest House Publishers, 2003), p. 68. See also Johnson, *Darwin on Trial*, p. 26; Charles Kingsley Levy, *Evolutionary Wars: A Three-Billion-Year Arms Race* (New York: W.H. Freeman and Company, 1999), p. 202.

17. See Jay Richards, "Darwinism and Design," *The Washington Post*, August 21, 1999, online edition.

18. Carl Wieland, "Goodbye, Peppered Moths," *Creation Ex Nihilo*, Vol. 21 No. 3, June-August 1999, p. 56.

19 John Morris, "Do Peppered Moths Prove Evolution?" *Back to Genesis*, No. 64b, April 1994, online edition.

20. See Johnson, *Darwin on Trial*, p. 25.

21. See Carl Wieland, "Darwin's Finches," *Creation Ex Nihilo*, Vol. 14 No. 3, June-August 1992, pp. 22-23.

22. Milton notes that "no one has ever bred a new species artificially—and both plant and animal breeders have been trying for hundreds of years, as have scientists" (Milton, p. 134).

23. Milton, pp. 141-42.

24. Lester, "Genetics: Enemy of Evolution."

25. Gary Parker, "Creation, Mutation, and Variation," *Impact*, No. 89, November 1980, Institute for Creation Research, online edition.

26. Gleason L. Archer, *Encyclopedia of Bible Difficulties* (Grand Rapids, MI: Zonderan, 1982), p. 56. See also Jerry Bergman, "Some Biological Problems with the Natural Selection Theory," *Creation Research Society Quarterly*, Vol. 29 No. 3, December 1992, online edition.

27. Charles Darwin, *On the Origin of Species* (New York: The Modern Library, 1856 reprint), p. 172; http://www.literaturepage.com/read/darwin-origin-of-species.html.

28. See Phillip E. Johnson, *Reason in the Balance: The Case Against Naturalism in Science, Law and Education* (Downers Grove, IL: InterVarsity Press, 1995), p. 81.

29. Richard Dawkins, *The Blind Watchmaker: Why the Evidence of Evolution Reveals a Universe Without Design* (New York: W.W. Norton, 1987), p. 5.

30. Mayr, p. 121.

31. H. J. Muller, "Radiation Damage to the Genetic Material," *American Scientist*, vol. 38 (Jan. 1950), p. 35.

32. Evolutionists themselves admit this. See Evans and Selina, p. 61.

33. Laurel Hicks, et. al., eds., *Science: Order and Reality* (Pensacola, FL: A Beka Book, 1993), p. 392.

34. Hugh Ross, *The Creator and the Cosmos* (Colorado Springs, CO: NavPress, 2001), p. 141.

35. See Jones, p. 111.

36. Milton, p. 155; see also Muncaster, p. 152.

37. See Johnson, *Darwin on Trial*, p. 32.

38. William A. Dembski, *Intelligent Design: The Bridge Between Science & Theology* (Downers Grove, IL: InterVarsity Press, 1999), p. 113.

Chapter 7—Comparative Anatomy, Vestigial Organs, and the Recapitulation Theory Do Not Prove Evolution

1. Richard Milton, *Shattering the Myths of Darwinism* (Rochester, VT: Park Street Press, 1997), p. 189.

2. Ernst Mayr argues that embryonic similarities, recapitulation, and vestigial structures raise "insurmountable problems" for creationists, but are fully compatible with evolution. As we will see, creationists argue precisely the opposite. See *What Evolution Is* (New York: Basic Books, 2001), p. 31.

3. Charles Darwin indicated his belief in this comparative anatomy argument, noting the similarity of various organs in different species. Interestingly, though, many of the naturalists of Darwin's day disagreed. "They recognized that according to the best principles of comparative anatomy, humans were close to apes and monkeys in almost all anatomical details, but the human mind was so utterly superior that the anatomists refused to group us with our animal cousins." Randal Keynes, *Annie's Box: Charles Darwin, His Daughter, and Human Evolution* (New York: Riverhead Books, 2001), p. 37.

4. See George F. Howe, "Homology and Origins," *Creation Matters*, Vol. 4 No. 5, September-October 1999, pp. 1, 3-5.

5. "Appendix," *Encyclopedia Britannica*, online edition.

6. "Appendix," *The Columbia Encyclopedia*, sixth ed., copyright 2002 Columbia University Press, online edition.

7. "Appendix," *Encarta Encyclopedia*, online edition.

8. Mayr, p. 31.

9. See Michael J. Behe, *Darwin's Black Box: The Biochemical Challenge to Evolution* (New York: The Free Press, 1996), p. 226.

10. See Ken Ham and Carl Wieland, "Your Appendix: It's There for a Reason," *Creation Ex Nihilo*, Vol. 20 No. 1, December 1997-February 1998, pp. 41-43. See also *Creation Matters*, Vol. 15 No. 4, July-August 2000, p. 7.

11. Henry M. Morris, *Scientific Creationism* (Green Forest, AR: Master Books, 2001), p. 76.

12. Norman L. Geisler, *Baker Encyclopedia of Christian Apologetics*, in The Norman Geisler CD-ROM Library (Grand Rapids, MI: Baker Book House, 2002). See also Don Batten, ed., *The Revised and Expanded Answers Book* (Green Forest, AR: Master Books, 1990), p. 122.

13. This information is derived from Milton, p. 188; Ham and Wieland, p. 2; "Quiz," *Creation Matters*, Vol. 5 No. 2, March-April 2000, 7; "Functional Appendix," *Creation Matters*, Vol. 6 No. 5, September-October 2001, p. 8.

14. Humans are not the only living beings with vestigial organs, according to evolutionists. Some have argued, for example, that the tiny muscles in horses' legs, attached to very long tendons, are vestigial. However, these muscles serve as a damper to reduce damage to bones when galloping, so they are not vestigial after all. See "Horses' 'Vestigial Muscles' Are Really Dampers," *Creation Matters*, Vol. 6 No. 6, November-December 2001, p. 7.

15. Dr. S.R. Scadding, department of zoology at the University of Guelph, Ontario; cited in Milton, p. 187.

16. Geisler, *Baker Encyclopedia of Christian Apologetics*.

17. *The Creation Hypothesis: Scientific Evidence for an Intelligent Designer* (Downers Grove, IL: InterVarsity Press, 1994), pp. 222-23. See also "The Appendix as Evidence for Evolution," *Creation Matters*, Vol. 2 No. 4, July-August 1997.

18. See Henry Morris, "The Heritage of the Recapitulation Theory," *Impact*, No. 183, September 1988, p. 1. See also "Haeckel, Ernst Heinrich (1834-1919)," *The Hutchinson Dictionary of Scientific Biography*, January 1, 1998, Electric Library.

19. Russell Grigg, "Fraud Rediscovered," *Creation Ex Nihilo*, Vol. 20 No. 2, March-May 1998, pp. 49-51, reproduced at Answers In Genesis website, www.answersingenesis.org.

20. "Does the Human Fetus Temporarily Develop Gills, a Tail, and a Yolk Sac?" Christian Answers website, www.christiananswers.net. (This is a reliable, well-respected website for strong apologetic answers to difficult issues. Some of my own material appears at this website.)

21. Dr. Spock, *Dr. Spock's Baby and Child Care*, p. 223; cited in Walter J. Bock, "Evolution by Orderly Law," *Science*, Vol. 164, May 9, 1969, pp. 684-85. "Does the Human Fetus Temporarily Develop Gills, a Tail, and a Yolk Sac?" Christian Answers website.

22. Mayr, p. 27.

23. Carl Sagan, "Is It Possible to Be Pro-Life and Pro-Choice?" *Parade Magazine*, April 22, 1990, p. 6.

24. See Wayne Friar, "Embryology and Evolution," *Creation Research Society Quarterly*, Vol. 36 No. 2, September 1999, pp. 1-2.

25. Friar, p. 1.

26. Grigg, "Fraud Rediscovered." See also Stephen Jay Gould, *I Have Landed: The End of a Beginning in Natural History* (New York: Harmony Books, 2002), p. 310.

27. Ralph O. Muncaster, *Dismantling Evolution* (Eugene, OR: Harvest House Publishers, 2003), p. 74.

28. Steve Jones, *Darwin's Ghost: The Origin of Species Updated* (New York: Random House, 2000), p. 298.

29. Michael Richardson, *Anatomy and Embryology*, Vol. 196 No. 2, 1997, pp. 91-106.

30. Grigg, "Fraud Rediscovered." See also Elizabeth Pennisi, "Haeckel's Embryos: Fraud Rediscovered," *Science*, September 5, 1997, Electric Library.

31. Michael Richardson, interviewed by Nigel Hawkes, *The Times*, August 11, 1997, p. 14; cited in Grigg, "Fraud Rediscovered."

32. Don Batten, ed., *The Revised and Expanded Answers Book* (Green Forest, AR: Master Books, 1990), p. 118; see also Friar, p. 3.

33. Gould, *I Have Landed*, p. 311; See also Jonathan Wells, "Survival of the Fakest Science," *The American Spectator*, December 1, 2000, Electric Library. Others agree with Gould. See G.G. Simpson and W. Beck, *An Introduction to Biology* (New York: Harcourt Brace and World, 1965), p. 241.

34. See Michael Richardson; cited in Gould, *I Have Landed*, p. 312.

35. See Milton, p. 189.

36. See Milton, p. 189.

Chapter 8—The Universe Is Intelligently Designed

1. William A. Dembski, *Intelligent Design: The Bridge Between Science & Theology* (Downers Grove, IL: InterVarsity Press, 1999), p. 126.

2. Michael J. Behe, William A. Dembski, and Stephen C. Meyer, *Science and Evidence for Design in the Universe* (San Francisco, CA: Ignatius Press, 2002), p. 53.

3. William A. Dembski and James M. Kushiner, eds., *Signs of Intelligence* (Grand Rapids, MI: Brazos Press, 2001), p. 48.

4. Dembski, *Intelligent Design*, p. 99.

5. Holly J. Morris, "Life's Grand Design," *U.S. News & World Report*, November 29, 2002, p. 52.

6. See, for example, Phillip E. Johnson, *Defeating Darwinism by Opening Minds* (Downers Grove, IL: InterVarsity Press, 1997), p. 23.

7. Dembski, *Intelligent Design*, p. 127.

8. William Paley, *Natural Theology: Or Evidences of the Existence and Attributes of the Deity, Collected from the Appearances of Nature*, Second Edition, vol. 1 (Oxford: J. Vincent, 1828), p. 65, inserts added.

9. Del Ratzsch, *The Battle of Beginnings: Why Neither Side Is Winning the Creation-Evolution Debate* (Downers Grove, IL: InterVarsity Press, 1996), p. 32.

10. Charles Darwin, *The Autobiography of Charles Darwin*, ed. Nora Darwin Barlow (New York: W.W. Norton, 1993), p. 162.

11. Charles Darwin, *On the Origin of Species* (New York: The Modern Library, 1856 reprint), p. 162; http://www.literaturepage.com/read/darwin-origin-of-species.html.

12. Behe, Dembski, and Meyer, p. 119.

13. Helen Fryman, "The Intelligent Design Movement," *Creation Matters*, Vol. 5 No. 2, March-April 2000, p. 4.

14. Michael Behe, "A Mousetrap Defended: Response to Critics," Discovery Institute, July 31, 2003; Michael Behe, "Blind Evolution or Intelligent Design: Address to the American Museum of Natural History," April 23, 2002, Discovery Institute website, www.discovery.org.

15. Behe, Dembski, and Meyer, p. 119.

16. *Signs of Intelligence*, p. 94.

17. See, for example, Joseph Paturi, "The Human Body—God's Masterpiece," *Creation Ex Nihilo*, Vol. 20 No. 4, September-November 1998, pp. 54-55.

18. See George Sim Johnston, "Designed for Living," *Wall Street Journal*, October 15, 1999, Discovery Institute website, www.discovery.org. See also Tom Wagner, "Darwin vs. the Eye," *Creation Ex Nihilo*, Vol. 16 No. 4, September-November 1994, pp. 10-13.

19. See Behe, Dembski, and Meyer, p. 116.

20. Jimmy H. Davis and Harry L. Poe, *Designer Universe: Intelligent Design and the Existence of God* (Nashville, TN: Broadman & Holman Publishers, 2002), p. 71. See also Ratzsch, p. 46.

21. See Michael Behe, "Molecular Machines: Experimental Support for the Design Inference," *Cosmic Pursuit*, March 1, 1998, Discovery Institute website, www.discovery.org.

22. *Webster's Revised Unabridged Dictionary* (MICRA, Inc. 1998), online edition.

23. Johnson, *Darwin on Trial*, p. 34.

24. Davis and Poe, p. 71.

25. See Johnson, *Darwin on Trial*, p. 35. See also Phillip E. Johnson, *Reason in the Balance: The Case Against Naturalism in Science, Law and Education* (Downers Grove, IL: InterVarsity Press, 1995), pp. 78-79.

26. See Johnson, *Reason in the Balance*, p. 81.

27. John C. Whitcomb, *The Early Earth* (Grand Rapids, MI: Baker Book House, 1979), p. 87.

28. Behe, Dembski, and Meyer, p. 117.

29. Dan Schobert, Book Review of Michael Behe's *Darwin's Black Box: The Biochemical Challenge to Evolution*, *Creation Matters*, Vol. 4 No. 6, November-December 1999, Creation Research Society website, www.creationresearch.org.

30. Johnson, *Defeating Darwinism by Opening Minds*, p. 77.

31. For example, Ernst Haeckel.

32. *Signs of Intelligence*, p. 93. See also Frank S. Salisbury, "Doubts about the Modern Synthetic Theory of Evolution," *American Biology Teacher* (September 1971), p. 336. In Henry M. Morris, *Scientific Creationism* (Green Forest, AR: Master Books, 2001), p. 62.

33. Despite overwhelming evidence, however, many biologists are reluctant to consider intelligent design as an option. See *The Creation Hypothesis: Scientific Evidence for an Intelligent Designer* (Downers Grove, IL: InterVarsity Press, 1994), p. 68.

34. *Signs of Intelligence*, p. 11.

35. Johnson, *Defeating Darwinism by Opening Minds*, p. 77.

36. *Signs of Intelligence*, p. 103.

37. Melinda Penkavia, "Analysis: Whether the Theory of Intelligent Design Should Be Taught in the Classroom," NPR, February 13, 2002, Electric Library.

38. Behe, Dembski, and Meyer, pp. 67-68. See also Behe, "Molecular Machines: Experimental Support for the Design Inference."

39. Norman Geisler and Joseph Holden, *Living Loud: Defending Your Faith* (Nashville, TN: Broadman & Holman Publishers, 2002), p. 56.

40. Richard Dawkins, *The Blind Watchmaker* (New York: W.W. Norton, 1996), p. 115.

41. Russell Grigg, "A Brief History of Design," *Creation Ex Nihilo*, Vol. 22 No. 2, March-May 2000, p. 52.

42. Like Windows 98, for example. Cyrus Farivar, "UC-Berkeley Scholars Weigh In On Challenge to Evolution," *University Wire*, March 11, 2002, Electric Library.

43. *Signs of Intelligence*, p. 115. Davis and Poe, pp. 202-03. See also Grigg, "A Brief History of Design."

44. Bill Gates, *The Road Ahead* (Boulder, CO: Blue Penguin, 1996), p. 228; in Behe, Dembski, and Meyer, p. 71. See also Jay Richards, "Intelligent Design Theory: Why It Matters," IntellectualCapital.com, July 25, 1999.

45. See Behe, Dembski, and Meyer, p. 92.

46. Behe, Dembski, and Meyer, p. 12. Dembski is careful to point out that intelligent design theorists do not invoke the book of Genesis (or any other biblical book), do not ascribe to a narrow hermeneutic in interpreting Scripture, and do not identify who the Designer might be (for example, God). Rather, design theory seeks to empirically demonstrate the scientific failure of Darwinism. See William Dembski, "What Every Theologian Should Know about Creation, Evolution, and Design," *The Princeton Theological Review*, April 1, 1996; Philip Gold, "Darwinism in Denial?" *Washington Times*, August 23, 2001, Discovery Institute website, www.discovery.org.

47. Davis and Poe, 115. Dembski, *Intelligent Design*, pp. 17, 128.

48. Dembski, *Intelligent Design*, p. 17.

49. Davis and Poe, p. 119.

50. Benjamin Wiker, "Does Science Point to God?: The Intelligent Design Revolution," *Crisis*, April 8, 2003, Discovery Institute website, www.discovery.org.

51. Robin Collins, "The Fine-Tuning Design Argument: A Scientific Argument for the Existence of God," *Reason for the Hope Within*, September 1, 1998, Discovery Institute website, www.discovery.org.

52. Collins, "The Fine-Tuning Design Argument."

53. Hugh Ross, *The Creator and the Cosmos* (Colorado Springs, CO: NavPress, 2001), p. 151.

54. Ross, p. 151.

55. Behe, Dembski, and Meyer, pp. 56-57.

56. Hank Hanegraaff, "The Failure of Evolution to Account for the Miracle of Life," *Christian Research Journal*, Summer 1998, online edition.

57. Robert Jastrow, *God and the Astronomers* (New York: W.W. Norton & Company, Inc., 1992), p. 118. A term has been coined to refer to the fact that the universe seems fine-tuned for the existence of human life: "the anthropic principle."

58. Fred Hoyle, "The Universe: Past and Present Reflections," *Annual Reviews of Astronomy and Astrophysics* 20 (1982), p. 16.

59. George Greenstein, *The Symbiotic Universe: Life and Mind in the Cosmos* (New York: Morrow, 1988), pp. 26-27.

60. See Dembski, *Intelligent Design*, p. 14. See also Henry Morris, "Design Is Not Enough!" *Back to Genesis*, No. 127a, July 1999, Creation Research Institute (www.icr.org); Fryman, p. 4.

61. *The American Heritage Dictionary of the English Language*, Fourth Edition (Houghton Mifflin Company, 2000), online edition.

62. See *The Creation Hypothesis*, p. 68.

63. Behe, Dembski, and Meyer, pp. 11-12.

Chapter 9—Evolutionist Objections to Intelligent Design Can Be Intelligently Answered

1. See Helen Fryman, "The Intelligent Design Movement," *Creation Matters*, Vol. 5 No. 2, March-April 2000, pp. 1, 3-5.

2. Holly Morris, "Life's Grand Design," *U.S. News & World Report*, July 29, 2002, p. 52.

3. Cyrus Farivar, "UC-Berkeley Scholars Weigh In On Challenge to Evolution," *University Wire*, March 11, 2002, Electric Library.

4. Melinda Penkava, "Analysis: Whether the Theory of Intelligent Design Should Be Taught in the Classroom," NPR, February 13, 2002, Electric Library.

5. See William A. Dembski and James M. Kushiner, eds., *Signs of Intelligence* (Grand Rapids, MI: Brazos Press, 2001), p. 116.

6. Michael Behe, lecture delivered at the American Museum of Natural History, April 23, 2002, transcript at Discovery Institute website, www.discovery.org, insert added.

7. Penkava, "Analysis: Whether the Theory of Intelligent Design Should Be Taught in the Classroom."

8. *The Creation Hypothesis: Scientific Evidence for an Intelligent Designer* (Downers Grove, IL: InterVarsity Press, 1994), p. 82.

9. Morris, "Life's Grand Design."

10. "Challenging Darwin," *The Washington Times*, September 19, 2002, Electric Library.

11. See William A. Dembski, *Intelligent Design: The Bridge Between Science & Theology* (Downers Grove, IL: InterVarsity Press, 1999), p. 257.

12. Dembski, *Intelligent Design*, p. 258.

13. *Signs of Intelligence*, p. 9.

14. Robin Collins, "The Fine-Tuning Design Argument: A Scientific Argument for the Existence of God," reprinted from *Reason for the Hope Within*, September 1, 1998, Discovery Institute website, www.discovery.org. See *Signs of Intelligence*, p. 12. Dembski, *Intelligent Design*, p. 261.

15. See William A. Dembski, "Intelligent Design Is Not Optimal Design," *Metaviews*, February 2, 2000, Discovery Institute website, www.discovery.org.

16. Charles Darwin, letter to Asa Gray, May 22, 1860.

17. Ken Boa and Larry Moody, *I'm Glad You Asked* (Colorado Springs, CO: Victor Books, 1994), p. 129.

18. Norman L. Geisler, *Baker Encyclopedia of Christian Apologetics* (Grand Rapids, MI: Baker Book House, 1999), p. 220.

19. Millard J. Erickson, *Introducing Christian Doctrine* (Grand Rapids, MI: Baker Book House, 1996), pp. 138-39.

20. Erickson, p. 139.

21. Norman L. Geisler and Ronald M. Brooks, *When Skeptics Ask* (Wheaton, IL: Victor Books, 1990), pp. 59-60.

22. Paul E. Little, *Know Why You Believe* (Downers Grove, IL: InterVarsity Press, 1975), p. 81.

23. Little, p. 81.

24. Geisler and Brooks, p. 73.

25. Little, p. 87.

26 Boa and Moody, p. 131.

27. Norman L. Geisler and Jeff Amanu, "Evil," in *New Dictionary of Theology*, eds. Sinclair B. Ferguson and David F. Wright (Downers Grove, IL: InterVarsity Press, 1988), p. 242.

28. Dan Story, *Defending Your Faith* (Nashville, TN: Thomas Nelson Publishers, 1992), pp. 171-72.

29. Geisler and Brooks, p. 73.

30. Geisler and Brooks, pp. 64-65.

31. R.E.D. Clark, *Darwin: Before and After* (London: Paternoster Press, 1948), p. 86.

32. Geisler and Brooks, p. 76.

33. Michael Behe, for example, is a Roman Catholic who is open to the idea that all organisms (man included) descended from a common ancestor over billions of years. His main emphasis is that there is evidence of design at the molecular level, and hence God had to have gotten things started. Darwinism cannot account for the complex molecules that make life tick.

34. Morris, "Life's Grand Design."

35. Farivar, "UC-Berkeley Scholars Weigh In On Challenge to Evolution."

36. "Challenging Darwin," *The Washington Times.*

37. See Carl Wieland, "AIG's Views on the Intelligent Design Movement," August 30, 2002, Answers in Genesis website.

38. Fryman, "The Intelligent Design Movement," p. 4.

Chapter 10—The "Big Bang" Theory May or May Not Be Compatible with Creationism

1. Hugh Ross, *The Creator and the Cosmos* (Colorado Springs, CO: NavPress, 2001), p. 32.

2. Robert Jastrow, *God and the Astronomers* (New York: W.W. Norton & Company, Inc., 1992), p. 12; see also pp. 28-29.

3. Jastrow, p. 12.

4. Norman L. Geisler and Ronald Brooks, *When Skeptics Ask*, The Norman Geisler CD-ROM Library (Grand Rapids, MI: Baker Book House, 2002).

5. Paul Recer, "Universe Found 13 Billion Years Old," *AP Online*, April 25, 2002; see also Jimmy H. Davis and Harry L. Poe, *Designer Universe: Intelligent Design and the Existence of God* (Nashville, TN: Broadman & Holman Publishers, 2002), pp. 80-81.

6. Jastrow, p. 13.

7. Dan Vergano, "NASA Peers Back to the Beginning of the Universe," *USA Today*, February 12, 2003, 10D; see also Paul Recer, "New Theory on Big Bang," *AP Online*, January 9, 2002.

8. Davis and Poe, pp. 80-81.

9. Jastrow, p. 55.

10. Michael Behe, *Darwin's Black Box: The Biochemical Challenge to Evolution* (New York: The Free Press, 1996), p. 244.

11. Ralph O. Muncaster, *Dismantling Evolution* (Eugene, OR: Harvest House Publishers, 2003), pp. 202-03.

12. British cosmologist Sir Arthur Eddington said the very idea was repugnant to him. See Ross, p. 77.

13. William A. Dembski, *Intelligent Design: The Bridge Between Science & Theology* (Downers Grove, IL: InterVarsity Press, 1999), pp. 204-05; Muncaster, p. 201.

14. Behe, p. 244.

15. Jastrow, p. 119.

16. "Scientists and Theologians Discover a Common Ground," *U.S. News and World Report*, July 20, 1998, p. 52.

17. Ross, p. 32.

18. Jeff Nesmith, "'Big-Bang' Theory Prompts Scientists, Theologians to Explore," *The Washington Times*, April 11, 1999, p. A1.

19. Design theorists point out that just a small increase in the rate of expansion of our universe—say, by one part in 10^{60}—would cause the universe to be too diffuse in matter to allow star formation. See Michael J. Behe, William A. Dembski, and Stephen C. Meyer, *Science and Evidence for Design in the Universe* (San Francisco, CA: Ignatius Press, 2002), p. 60. See also Ross, p. 151.

20. See Frank Roylance, "Was God Present at the Creation?" *The Toronto Star*, May 2, 1999, Electric Library.

21. See Ross, p. 28.

22. R. C. H. Lenski, *Hebrews* (Minneapolis, MN: Augsburg Publishing House, 1961), p. 36.

23. F. F. Bruce, *The Epistle to the Hebrews* (Grand Rapids, MI: Eerdmans, 1979), p. 4.

24. John MacArthur, *The Superiority of Christ* (Chicago, IL: Moody Press, 1986), p. 33.

25 Harold B. Kuhn, "Creation," in Carl F. Henry, ed., *Basic Christian Doctrines* (Grand Rapids, MI: Baker Book House, 1983), p. 61.

26. Louis Berkhof, *Manual of Christian Doctrine* (Grand Rapids, MI: Wm. B. Eerdmans Publishing Co., 1983), p. 96.

27. Henry Morris, *The Biblical Basis for Modern Science* (Grand Rapids, MI: Baker Book House, 1984), p. 172.

28. Morris, p. 172.

29 Morris, p. 172.

30. Morris, p. 151.

31. Duane Gish, "The Big Bang Theory Collapses," *Impact*, No 216, June 1991; see also John Morris, "Has the Big Bang Been Saved?" *Back to Genesis*, No. 42b, June 1992, both articles at Institute for Creation Research website,www.icr.org.

32 Dr. Werner Gitt, *Creation Ex Nihilo*, Vol. 20 No. 3, June-August 1998, pp. 42-44.

33. Gish, "The Big Bang Theory Collapses." Note that astronomers respond by arguing that the COBE satellite has measured small fluctuations in background radiation, but it was only 30 millionths of a degree, an insignificant variation. See Morris, "Has the Big Bang Been Saved?"

34. See Henry Morris, "The Cosmic Bubbleland," *Back to Genesis*, No. 150a, June 2001, Institute for Creation Research website,www.icr.org.

35. See Henry Morris, "The Coming Big Bang," *Back to Genesis*, No. 101a, May 1997, Institute for Creation Research website,www.icr.org; see also Ira Flatow, "Interview: Paul Steinhardt Discusses an Alternate Theory on How the Universe Began," *Talk of the Nation*, NPR, May 17, 2002; Fred Guterl, "The Creation Equation," *Newsweek International*, May 28, 2001, p. 55; "New Findings Support Inflationary Universe," United Press International, May 23, 2002, Electric Library; Matt Bell, "No More Big Bang? Stanford U. Research Presents New Beginning to Universe," *University Wire*, February 11, 1999.

36 See, for example, Gregg Easterbrook, "What Came Before Creation?" *U.S. News and World Report*, July 20, 1998, p. 44.

37. Henry Morris, "What Astronomers Don't Know," *Back to Genesis*, No. 163, July 7, 2002, Institute for Creation Research website,www.icr.org.

38. For example, the science involved in intelligent design theory is extremely persuasive.

Appendix—The Second Law of Thermodynamics Argues Against Evolution

1. Isaac Asimov, "In the Game of Energy and Thermodynamics, You Can't Even Break Even," *Smithsonian* (June 1970), p. 6.

2. Asimov, p. 10.

3. Henry M. Morris, "Seven Reasons for Opposing Evolution," *Bibliotheca Sacra* (Dallas, TX: Dallas Theological Seminary [Electronic edition by Galaxie Software]) 1999.

4. Del Ratzsch, *The Battle of Beginnings: Why Neither Side Is Winning the Creation-Evolution Debate* (Downers Grove, IL: InterVarsity Press, 1996), p. 91.

5. Charles Ryrie, *Basic Theology* (Wheaton, IL: Victor Books, 1986), p. 177.

6. Morris, "Seven Reasons for Opposing Evolution." See also Norman Geisler and Thomas Howe, *When Critics Ask: A Popular Handbook on Bible Difficulties*, The Norman Geisler CD-ROM Library (Grand Rapids, MI: Baker Book House), 2002.

7. Lincoln Barnett, *The Universe and Dr. Einstein* (New York: Amereon Ltd., 1950), pp. 102-03, insert added.

8. Robert Jastrow, *God and the Astronomers* (New York: W.W. Norton & Company, Inc., 1992), p. 33.

9. John C. Whitcomb, *The Early Earth* (Grand Rapids, MI: Baker Book House, 1979), p. 12.

10. J.W.N. Sullivan, *The Limitations of Science* (New York: Augustus M. Kelley Publishers, 1930), p. 24.

11. Whitcomb, 56.

12. See Henry Morris, *The Biblical Basis for Modern Science* (Grand Rapids, MI: Baker Book House, 1984), p. 190.

13. This possibility is suggested by Robert Hill, "Did Entropy Change Before the Curse?" *Creation Matters*, September/October 2001, pp. 6-7.

14. Merrill F. Unger, *Beyond the Crystal Ball* (Chicago, IL: Moody Press, 1973), p. 173.

15. See Ron Rhodes, *Christ Before the Manger: The Life and Times of the Preincarnate Christ* (Eugene, OR: Wipf & Stock Publishers, 2002), chapter 12.

Bibliography

Batten, Don, ed. *The Revised and Expanded Answers Book*. Green Forest, AR: Master Books, 2000.

Behe, Michael, William A. Dembski, and Stephen C. Meyer. *Science and Evidence for Design in the Universe*. San Francisco: Ignatius Press, 2002.

Behe, Michael. *Darwin's Black Box*. New York: The Free Press, 1996.

Caird, Rod. *Ape Man: The Story of Human Evolution*. New York: MacMillan, 1994.

Craig, William Lane. "Philosophical and Scientific Pointers to Creatio Ex Nihilo." *Journal of the American Scientific Affiliation*. 32 (March 1980): 5-13.

———. "The Existence of God." In *Reasonable Faith: Christian Truth and Apologetics*. Wheaton, IL: Crossway, 1994.

———. *The Existence of God and the Beginning of the Universe*. San Bernardino, CA: Here's Life Publishers, 1979.

Davis, Jimmy H., and Harry L. Poe. *Designer Universe: Intelligent Design and the Existence of God*. Nashville, TN: Broadman & Holman, 2002.

Dawkins, Richard. *The Blind Watchmaker: Why the Evidence of Evolution Reveals a Universe Without Design*. New York: W.W. Norton, 1996.

Dembski, William A., ed. *Mere Creation: Science, Faith and Intelligent Design*. Downers Grove, IL: InterVarsity Press, 1998.

———. *Intelligent Design: The Bridge Between Science & Theology*. Downers Grove, IL: InterVarsity Press, 1999.

———. *The Design Inference: Eliminating Chance Through Small Probabilities*. Cambridge: Cambridge University Press, 1998.

Dembski, William A., and James M. Kushiner, eds. *Signs of Intelligence: Understanding Intelligent Design*. Grand Rapids, MI: Brazos Press, 2001.

Denton, Michael. *Evolution: A Theory in Crisis*. Bethesda, MD: Adler and Adler, 1985.

Evans, Dylan, and Howard Selina. *Introducing Evolution*. Cambridge: Totem Books, 2001.

Fortey, Richard. *Life: A Natural History of the First Four Billion Years of Life on Earth*. New York: Alfred A. Knopf, 1997.

Geisler, Norman L. *Baker Encyclopedia of Christian Apologetics*. Grand Rapids, MI: Baker Book House, 1999.

———., and Ron Brooks. *When Skeptics Ask: A Handbook on Christian Evidences*. Wheaton, IL: Victor Books, 1990.

———., and Thomas Howe. *When Critics Ask: A Popular Handbook on Bible Difficulties*. Wheaton, IL: Victor Books, 1992.

Gish, Duane. *Evolution: The Challenge of the Fossil Record*. El Cajon, CA: Creation-Life Publishers, 1985.

Gould, Stephen Jay. *I Have Landed: The End of a Beginning in Natural History*. New York: Harmony Books, 2002.

———, ed. *The Book of Life: An Illustrated History of the Evolution of Life on Earth*. New York: W.W. Norton, 2001.

Hanegraaff, Hank. *The Face that Demonstrates the Farce of Evolution*. Nashville, TN: W Publishing Group, 1998.

Jastrow, Robert. *God and the Astronomers*. New York: W.W. Norton, 1992.

Johnson, Phillip. *Darwin On Trial*. Downers Grove, IL: InterVarsity Press, 1993.

———. *Defeating Darwinism by Opening Minds*. Downers Grove, IL: InterVarsity Press, 1997.

———. *Reason in the Balance: The Case Against Naturalism in Science, Law and Education*. Downers Grove, IL: InterVarsity Press, 1995.

Jones, Steve. *Darwin's Ghost: The Origin of Species Updated*. New York: Random House, 2000.

Jordan, Paul. *Neanderthal: Neanderthal Man and the Story of Human Origins*. Great Britain: Sutton Publishing, 1999.

Keynes, Randal. *Darwin, His Daughter, and Human Evolution*. New York: Riverhead Books, 2001.

Leakey, Richard. *The Origin of Humankind*. New York: Basic Books, 1994.

Levy, Charles Kingsley. *Evolutionary Wars: A Three-Billion-Year Arms Race*. New York: W.H. Freeman and Company, 1999.

Lubenow, Marvin L. *Bones of Contention: A Creationist Assessment of Human Fossils*. Grand Rapids, MI: Baker Book House, 1992.

Mayr, Ernst. *What Evolution Is*. New York: Basic Books, 2001.

Miethe, Terry L., and Gary R. Habermas. *Why Believe God Exists! Rethinking the Case for God and Christianity*. Joplin, MO: College Press, 1993.

Moreland, J.P., ed. *The Creation Hypothesis*. Downers Grove, IL: InterVarsity Press, 1994.

Moreland, J.P., and John Mark Reynolds, eds. *Three Views of Creation and Evolution*. Grand Rapids, MI: Zondervan, 1999.

Morris, Henry M. *That Their Words May Be Used Against Them*. Green Forest, AR: Master Books, 1997.

———. *The Troubled Waters of Evolution*. San Diego, CA: Creation-Life Publishers, 1974.

———, ed. *Scientific Creationism*. San Diego, CA: Creation-Life Publishers, 1974.

Ratzsch, Del. *The Battle of Beginnings*. Downers Grove, IL: InterVarsity Press, 1996.

Rhodes, Ron. *Christ Before the Manger: The Life and Times of the Preincarnate Christ*. Eugene, OR: Wipf and Stock Publishers, 2003.

———. *Miracles Around Us*. Eugene, OR: Harvest House Publishers, 2000.

———. *The Complete Book of Bible Answers*. Eugene, OR: Harvest House Publishers, 1997.

Ridley, Mark, ed. *Evolution*. Oxford: Oxford University Press, 1997.

Ross, Hugh. *The Creator and the Cosmos*. Colorado Springs, CO: NavPress, 2001.

———. *The Creator and the Cosmos: How the Greatest Scientific Discoveries of the Century Reveal God*. Colorado Springs, CO: NavPress, 1993.

Schopf, J. William. *Evolution: Facts and Fallacies*. San Diego, CA: Academic Press, 1999.

Shapiro, Robert. *Origins: A Skeptic's Guide to the Creation of Life on Earth*. New York: Summit Books, 1986.

Strathern, Paul. *The Big Idea: Crick, Watson, and DNA*. New York: Anchor Books, 1997.

Thaxton, Charles B., Walter L. Bradley, and Roger L. Olsen. *The Mystery of Life's Origin: Reassessing Current Theories*. New York: Philosophical Library, 1984.

Wade, Nicholas. *The Science Times Book of Fossils and Evolution*. New York: The Lyons Press, 1998.

Wilder-Smith, A.E. *Man's Origin, Man's Destiny: A Critical Survey of the Principles of Evolution and Christianity*. Minneapolis, MN: Bethany House Publishers, 1968.

———, A.E. *The Creation of Life: A Cybernetic Approach to Evolution*. Costa Mesa, CA: TWFT Publishers, 1970.

———, A.E. *The Natural Sciences Know Nothing of Evolution*. Costa Mesa, CA: TWFT Publishers, 1981.

———, A.E. *The Scientific Alternative to Neo-Darwinian Evolutionary Theory: Information Sources and Structures*. Costa Mesa, CA: TWFT Publishers, 1987.